READING GROUP CHOICES
⌒ 2023 ⌒

Selections for lively discussions

Reading Group Choices' goal is to join with publishers, bookstores, libraries, trade associations, and authors to develop resources to enhance the shared reading group experience. *Reading Group Choices* is distributed annually to bookstores, libraries, and directly to book groups. Titles included in the current and previous issues are posted on ReadingGroupChoices.com. Books presented here have been recommended by book group members, librarians, booksellers, literary agents, publicists, authors, and publishers. All submissions are then reviewed to ensure the discussibility of each title. Once a title is approved for inclusion, publishers are asked to underwrite production costs so that copies of *Reading Group Choices* can be distributed for a minimal charge. For additional copies, you can place an order through our online store, contact us, or contact your local library or bookstore. For more information, please visit our website at **ReadingGroupChoices.com.**

Cover art, *Reader* by Carson Ellis (2018)
Design by Kate Thomfohrda

Copyright © 2023 Reading Group Choices LLC

All Rights Reserved.

Published in the United States by Reading Group Choices LLC

ISBN 9781733268363

For further information, contact:
Reading Group Choices
info@ReadingGroupChoices.com
ReadingGroupChoices.com

PRAISE FOR *READING GROUP CHOICES*

"We have learned over the years that displays are a great way to encourage circulation at our small, rural library. One of our best displays is based on the wonderful literary guide published by Reading Group Choices! ... Patrons cannot wait to get their copies and start reading. We sincerely LOVE your product and feel that it helps us create one of our favorite displays EVER."
—**Gail Nartker, Sandusky District Library**

"Reading Group Choices continues to be a first-rate guide for those delicious reads that book group members enjoy reading, and that prompt the most enriching discussions." —**Donna Paz Kaufman, Paz & Associates, The Bookstore Training Group**

"I recommend Reading Group Choices as the number one starting point for book clubs. The newsletter is fantastic, and I especially like the Spotlight Book Club section. It is a nice way to meet other book clubs. I am very happy with the book selections offered by Reading Group Choices. Thank you for this excellent service." —**Ana Martin, Cover to Cover Book Club, Hollywood, FL**

"Not only is Reading Group Choices a great resource for individual readers and book groups, it's also an invaluable tool for teachers looking to introduce new books into their curriculum. Reading Group Choices is a brilliant concept, well executed." —**Kathleen Rourke, Executive Director of Educational Sales and Marketing, Candlewick Press**

"I love your book, website and the newsletters! As an organizer of two book clubs, it's so great to get an early line on upcoming titles. The hardest part is waiting so long to read the book! By using recommendations from your newsletters, I can build a list of monthly book selections one whole year in advance." —**Marcia, CCSI Book Club**

"Quail Ridge Books has worked with Reading Group Choices for many years and the guide has been sought out at our twice yearly Book Club Bash. The prize bags of books have been a highlight. We are great partners in getting good books into the hands of people who love to read and discuss books."
—**René Martin, Former Events Coordinator, Quail Ridge Books**

Welcome to
READING GROUP CHOICES

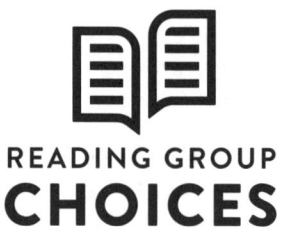

"Some of these things are true and some of them lies. But they are all good stories."

—**Hilary Mantel**

Dear Readers,

Welcome to the 29th edition of Reading Group Choices!

Each year we aim to include a variety of books on a range of topics that offer multiple avenues for discussion. We are always excited to see the new books that have been published and the books that are yet to come. We often find ourselves thinking, "Wow, this is a terrific edition" or sometimes we even think, "Maybe this is the best edition!" But, we are beginning to realize that maybe every year's edition is quite terrific, because every year new authors are writing amazing new books, and established authors are continuing to write and inspire us anew. And, well, all of that is pretty wonderful to look forward to, and to experience, and to spend some time talking about.

We are so pleased that we can continue to offer these new recommendations and resources for our fellow readers. What a wonderful world of books we are lucky enough to live in.

This 29th edition includes a variety of fiction, nonfiction, and young adult titles from a range of authors. We hope these titles will inspire many thoughtful, interesting, fun, and important discussions.

Some books are available now and some will be available in 2024 so you can plan ahead. There are longer versions of the conversation starters available online in our searchable database, along with author interviews and excerpts. Be sure to sign up for our eNewsletter, where you can find out about new monthly recommendations and giveaways as well as other resources for your groups.

To order more copies of this edition or past editions, visit our store online at www.ReadingGroupChoices.com.

We hope you enjoy another year of discovering, sharing, reading, and, most importantly, discussing new favorite books!

Mary Morgan & the Reading Group Choices Team

Contents

FICTION

Abyss, Pilar Quintana 12

An American Beauty, Shana Abé 14

Bewilderment, Richard Powers. 16

The Book Spy, Alan Hlad. 18

The Book Woman's Daughter, Kim Michele Richardson 20

Chasing the Black Eagle, Bruce Geddes. 22

Cocoon, Zhang Yueran 24

Cradles of the Reich, Jennifer Coburn 26

The Dark Queens, Shelley Puhak 28

Dr. No, Percival Everett 30

Dust Child, Nguyên Phan Quê Mai 32

The Family Chao, Lan Samantha Chang 34

Ghost Eaters, Clay McLeod Chapman 36

Half-Blown Rose, Leesa Cross-Smith. 38

In the Time of Our History, Susanne Pari 40

The Lies I Tell, Julie Clark 42

The Lost Girls of Willowbrook, Ellen Marie Wiseman 44

Maame, Jessica George 46

Moonrise Over New Jessup, Jamila Minnicks. 48

The Mystery of Mrs. Christie, Marie Benedict. 50

The Nurse's Secret, Amanda Skenandore 52

The Puppeteer's Daughters, Heather Newton 54

Seven Days in June, Tia Williams. 56

Shutter, Ramona Emerson. 58

The Ski Jumpers, Peter Geye 60

The Storyteller's Death, Ann Dávila Cardinal *62*

Such a Pretty Girl, Tammy Greenwood *64*

Take the Long Way Home, Rochelle Alers *66*

Tale of the Dreamer's Son, Preeta Samarasan *68*

Undesirables, Aomar Boum *70*

The Ways We Hide, Kristina McMorris *72*

NONFICTION

Animal Joy, Nuar Alsadir *76*

The Confidante, Christopher C. Gorham *78*

Helltown, Casey Sherman *80*

Last to Eat, Last to Learn: My Life in Afghanistan Fighting to Educate Women, Pashtana Durrani, Tamara Bralo *82*

The Red Widow: The Scandal that Shook Paris and the Woman Behind it All, Sarah Horowitz *84*

Seven Aunts, Staci Lola Drouillard *86*

Uncommon Measure: A Journey Through Music, Performance, and the Science of Time, Natalie Hodges *88*

Voice of the Fish: A Lyric Essay, Lars Horn *90*

Walk Through Fire: The Train Disaster that Changed America, Yasmine S. Ali, MD *92*

Your Hearts, Your Scars, Adina Talve-Goodman *94*

YOUNG ADULT

An Arrow to the Moon, Emily X.R. Pan *98*

As Long as the Lemon Trees Grow, Zoulfa Katouh *100*

The Elephant Girl, James Patterson and Ellen Banda-Aaku *102*

Fight Back, A.M. Dassu *104*

Merci Suárez Plays It Cool, Meg Medina *106*

The Silence That Binds Us, Joanna Ho *108*

The Sky We Shared, Shirley Reva Vernick *110*

Snitchers, Stephane Dunn *112*

Walls, L.M. Elliot *114*

What's Coming to Me, Francesca Padilla *116*

FICTION

ABYSS

Pilar Quintana, Lisa Dillman (Translator)

Longlisted for the 2023 National Book Award in Translated Literature

Claudia is an impressionable eight-year-old girl, trying to understand the world through the eyes of the adults around her. But her hardworking father hardly speaks a word, while her unhappy mother spends her days reading celebrity lifestyle magazines, tending to her enormous collection of plants, and filling Claudia's head with stories about women who end their lives in tragic ways. Then an interloper arrives, disturbing the delicate balance of family life, and Claudia's world starts falling apart. In this strikingly vivid portrait of Cali, Colombia, Claudia's acute observations remind us that children are capable of discerning extremely complex realities even if they cannot fully understand them.

"An eight-year-old girl takes in a series of troubling events in this luminous and transfixing account of fractured family life from Colombian writer Quintana (*The Bitch*). Readers will be dazzled." —*Publishers Weekly*, **Starred Review**

"Pilar Quintana has created a powerful story that contrasts with the hopeless and doomed atmosphere that surrounds the protagonist. In subtle and brilliant prose, in which nature connects us with the symbolic possibilities of literature, the abysses are both real and intimate." —Jury, **Alfaguara Novel Prize 2021**

ABOUT THE AUTHOR: **Pilar Quintana** is a widely respected Colombian author. Her previous novel, *The Bitch*, won a PEN Translates award in the UK and was a finalist for the National Book Award in the US. It also won the prestigious Colombian Biblioteca de Narrativa Prize, was selected for several Best Books of 2017 lists, and was chosen as one of the most valuable objects to preserve for future generations in a marble time capsule in Bogotá. *Abyss*, her latest novel, was awarded the Premio Alfaguara de Novela, which is among the most prestigious awards in the Spanish language.

February 2023 | Paperback | $17.99 | 9781642861228 | World Editions

CONVERSATION STARTERS

1. The mother and daughter in the story both have the same name: Claudia. What, if anything, do you think is the relevance of this?

2. House plants feature vividly in the book, both in the apartment of our protagonists (where they are referred to as the jungle) and in the home of Gloria Iné. What do you think these plants mean for the main characters: for the two women; for child-Claudia; for the father?

3. How many different abysses can you find within the novel, and how, if at all, are they negotiated?

4. Mother-Claudia is suffering from depression. What are its causes? What are its solutions? Who is to blame?

5. Can you see love in the novel? Do Claudia's parents love each other? Do they love Claudia? Where do you see this? Are there any other instances of love in the story?

6. What do you see for Claudia's future? Is it more hopeful than perhaps her mother's was?

7. What do you think about all the female deaths alluded to in the book? Were they accidents, or something else?

8. Why do you think Claudia's mother chooses to see these events in the way she does? (How) does it help her?

9. What happened to Gonzales? Both his entry into and exit out of the novel remain obscure—what was his agenda do you think?

10. Claudia's father is a man of few words, yet Claudia refers a number of times to the "monster" inside him. Does he appear more kind or more controlling to you?

11. Why did mother Claudia's job fail?

12. What does this story make you think about the rights and expectations of women in Colombian society? How does it compare with your own unbringing/environment?

13. It is clear that the women in this book suffer, but do you think the men suffer too? And if so, how?

14. This book is set in the 1980s—do you think things have changed?

AN AMERICAN BEAUTY
Shana Abé

Amidst the opulent glamor and vicious social circles of Gilded Age New York, this stunning biographical novel by the *New York Times* bestselling author of *The Second Mrs. Astor* conjures the true rags-to-riches story of Arabella Huntington. A woman whose great beauty was surpassed only by her exceptional business acumen, grit, and artistic eye, she defied the constraints of her era to become the wealthiest self-made woman in America.

1867, Richmond, Virginia: When they meet, Arabella is seventeen, beautiful, and impoverished, working at a disreputable gambling parlor in post-Civil War Richmond. Railroad baron Collis Potter Huntington is extremely wealthy, *quite* married, and nearly three decades her senior. But he is irresistibly drawn to this Southern girl with grit. Eventually, Arabella and her son move to New York, much closer to the mansion where Collis lives with his ailing wife. Using Collis's seed money and her own shrewd investing instincts, she begins to amass a fortune.

This single mother with mysterious origins would become the richest woman in America, a prescient businesswoman and art collector, a prominent philanthropist, and an outcast barred by the Astors and Vanderbilts from New York society. A woman ahead of her time, her story is one of reinvention, secrecy, brilliance, and grit – now brought to life in this captivating work of historical fiction.

"Abé is an exquisite storyteller." —**Fiona Davis**, *New York Times* bestselling author of *The Magnolia Palace*

"This story of one woman's ascent offers a fascinating look at the choices she made to become a Gilded Age titan." — *Kirkus Reviews*

ABOUT THE AUTHOR: **Shana Abé** is the award-winning, *New York Times*, *Wall Street Journal*, and *USA Today* bestselling author of more than a dozen novels, including *The Second Mrs. Astor* and *An American Beauty*. She lives in the mountains of Colorado and can be found online at ShanaAbe.com.

April 2023 | Paperback | $16.95 | 9781496739421 | Kensington

CONVERSATION STARTERS

1. Why do you think Arabella becomes romantically involved with a married man who is nearly three decades years her senior? Do you believe she loved him? How were her feelings for him different from her later feelings for Edward?

2. Do you think Belle still would have flourished as she did if she'd never met Collis? Would she have risen to such wealth? Why or why not?

3. What do you think of Arabella's efforts to manipulate Collis into moving her entire family from Richmond to New York, instead of just agreeing to his proposition at once and going by herself? Were her actions justified? Why do you think she risked so much to ensure her family would not be left behind?

4. What do you think of Collis's marriage to his first wife, Elizabeth? Did he love her? How was the power she held over him different from Arabella's power over him?

5. In what ways do you think Elizabeth punished Arabella for the open affair she had with her husband? Were her acts justified or fair?

6. Would you say that Arabella was a good mother to Archer? Why or why not?

7. Would you describe Arabella's rags-to-riches story as a "Cinderella" tale? What parallels are there, and where do the two stories diverge?

8. Who or what do you think was the true love of Arabella's life?

9. How does Belle choose to wield her power differently from the other elite women of New York? How are her values and priorities different from theirs? How are they similar?

10. Discuss Arabella's life from a feminist standpoint. In what ways did she promote feminist ideals? In what ways was she a victim of the society of her times?

11. Discuss the title of this book. What role did "beauty" play in Arabella's life?

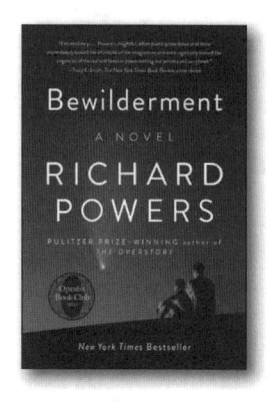

BEWILDERMENT

Richard Powers

An Oprah's Book Club Selection

A heartrending new novel from the Pulitzer Prize–winning and #1 *New York Times* best-selling author of *The Overstory*.

The astrobiologist Theo Byrne searches for life throughout the cosmos while single-handedly raising his unusual nine-year-old, Robin, following the death of his wife. Robin is a warm, kind boy who spends hours painting elaborate pictures of endangered animals. He's also about to be expelled from third grade for smashing his friend in the face. As his son grows more troubled, Theo hopes to keep him off psychoactive drugs. He learns of an experimental neurofeedback treatment to bolster Robin's emotional control, one that involves training the boy on the recorded patterns of his mother's brain.

With its soaring descriptions of the natural world, its tantalizing vision of life beyond, and its account of a father and son's ferocious love, *Bewilderment* marks Richard Powers's most intimate and moving novel. At its heart lies the question: How can we tell our children the truth about this beautiful, imperiled planet?

"Richard Powers is one of our country's greatest living writers. He composes some of the most beautiful sentences I've ever read. I'm in awe of his talent."
—**Oprah Winfrey**

"[A]stounding....a must-read novel....It's urgent and profound and takes readers on a unique journey that will leave them questioning what we're doing to the only planet we have."—**Rob Merril**, *Associated Press*

ABOUT THE AUTHOR: **Richard Powers** is the author of thirteen novels, including *The Overstory* and *Orfeo*, and the recipient of a MacArthur Fellowship, the Pulitzer Prize, and the National Book Award.

November 2022 | Paperback | $17.95 | 9781324036142 | W. W. Norton & Company

CONVERSATION STARTERS

1. *Bewilderment* opens with Robin's question about life on other planets—But we might never find them? (1). How does this question apply to the novel's concerns, extraterrestrial and otherwise? In what ways does it establish the scope of the novel's interests?

2. "Multiply every grain of sand on Earth by the number of trees. One hundred octillion" (8). This is how Theo describes the number of stars in the universe to Robin, and it's one of many ways Richard Powers illustrates the enormity of the natural world. What are some other examples that stood out to you? Why did they have an impact?

3. When Theo and Robin encounter a bear traffic jam in the Smokies, Theo thinks, "Our species had grown so desperate for alien contact that traffic could back up for miles at the fleeting glimpse of anything smart and wild" (36). How is this idea played out elsewhere in the novel? Have you ever seen a similar encounter in real life?

4. Powers frequently opens the book's sections with Theo and Robin contemplating distant, hypothetical planets. How do these alternative worlds give shape to each section? To the novel as a whole? In what ways are the questions they pose followed through in the plot?

5. We learn the circumstances of Alyssa's death gradually over the first half of the novel. What ambiguities does Powers introduce around the incident? Why do you think he reveals the details slowly?

6. Why does Theo resist putting Robin on prescription drugs for his behavioral issues? How do you interpret his resistance: stubborn, unrealistic, farsighted, rational? Did the end of the novel affect the way you interpret Theo's choice?

7. Several months into Robin's neurofeedback training, Theo worries that the treatment could be hurting his son. "In the face of the world's basic brokenness, more empathy meant deeper suffering" (138). Do you think the novel as a whole agrees or disagrees with this idea? Is the question left open?

THE BOOK SPY
ALAN HLAD

Based on the true stories of WWII's heroic librarian spies!

A New York Public Library archivist is fated to meet a Portuguese bookseller in wartime Lisbon, a city of espionage, in *USA Today* bestselling author Alan Hlad's love letter to the unique power of book people.

1942: Maria Alves longs to serve her country and honor the memory of her mother, a photojournalist killed by crossfire while covering the Spanish Civil War. As a microfilm expert at the New York Public Library who's fluent in six languages, she knows her best chance to continue her mother's fight against fascism is President Roosevelt's unlikely new taskforce of librarians in espionage. Soon after executing a mission of her own, she lands a spot within the Office of Strategic Services and is dispatched to the neutral city of Lisbon.

In Portugal, Maria poses as an American official collecting materials for the Library of Congress, visiting Lisbon's bookstores and news dealers to acquire Axis publications. It is in one such shop that she meets Tiago Soares, a Portuguese bookstore owner on a dangerous mission of his own: providing Jewish refugees with forged passports and visas to gain ship passage to the US.

United in their fight against the tyranny of evil and their shared love of the written word, Maria and Tiago grow close. But any future together is jeopardized when Maria's superiors send her on a new mission that will plunge her into the very heart of the Fuhrer's inner circle...

ABOUT THE AUTHOR: **Alan Hlad** is the internationally bestselling author of historical fiction novels inspired by real people and events of WWI and WWII, including *The Book Spy*, *Churchill's Secret Messenger*, *A Light Beyond the Trenches*, and the *USA Today* and IndieBound bestseller *The Long Flight Home*. A member of the Historical Novel Society, Literary Cleveland, Novelitics, and the Akron Writers' Group, he is a frequent speaker at conferences, literary events, and book club gatherings. He currently divides his time between Ohio and Portugal and can be found online at AlanHlad.com.

January 2023 | Paperback | $16.95 | 9781496738547 | Kensington Books

CONVERSATION STARTERS

1. *The Book Spy* is inspired by the very real but largely underrecognized librarians who served as intelligence agents during World War II. Before reading this novel, did you have much knowledge of how librarians contributed to the war effort? How did your prior knowledge—or lack thereof—affect your interest in this storyline?

2. Why did Colonel Donovan decide librarians and microfilm specialists would be best suited to serve as agents for the Interdepartmental Committee for the Acquisition of Foreign Publications? Are there any ordinary activities you perform in your job on a regular basis that you think would be well suited to an intelligence agent?

3. During WWII, Lisbon, Portugal was considered the last gate out of Europe for people fleeing Nazi persecution. An estimated one million refugees fled there to acquire ship passage to the United States, Canada, or Latin America. Before reading *The Book Spy*, were you aware of Portugal's significance in this regard? What did you learn from the novel about the experiences of Jewish refugees who escaped German-occupied Europe through the neutral port of Lisbon?

4. The character of Maria was inspired by Adele Kibre, an American archivist with a PhD in medieval linguistics who was recruited to the Interdepartmental Committee for the Acquisition of Foreign Publications (IDC) and stationed in Stockholm during WWII. Intelligent, brave, and not afraid to break the rules, Kibre was an expert in microphotography, fluent in 7 languages, and was—according to records—the most accomplished of the IDC agents. Despite her achievements and heroism, few people have heard of Adele Kibre. Why do you think there isn't more awareness of Adele Kibre and other librarians who served as intelligence agents?

5. There are many women from the past, like Adele Kibre, who do not often make it into our history books. Who is one woman from history that you greatly admire and think that the world should know more about?

6. While working in Lisbon, Maria and Tiago fall in love. What do you think brings them together? Why does their relationship develop so quickly? At what point do you think Maria realized she loved Tiago? How is the war a catalyst for their affection?

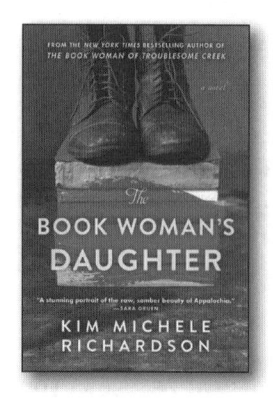

THE BOOK WOMAN'S DAUGHTER

Kim Michele Richardson

The instant *New York Times* bestseller!

As the daughter of the famed blue-skinned, Troublesome Creek packhorse librarian, Honey and her family have been hiding from the law all her life. But when her mother and father are imprisoned, Honey realizes she must fight to stay free, or risk being sent away for good.

Picking up her mother's old packhorse library route, Honey begins to deliver books to the remote hollers of Appalachia. Honey is looking to prove that she doesn't need anyone telling her how to survive. But the route can be treacherous, and some folks aren't as keen to let a woman pave her own way.

If Honey wants to bring the freedom books provide to the families who need it most, she's going to have to fight for her place, and along the way, learn that the extraordinary women who run the hills and hollers can make all the difference in the world.

"A powerful portrait of the courageous women." —**William Kent Krueger,** *New York Times* **bestselling author of** *This Tender Land* **and** *Lightning Strike*

"A critical and profoundly important read for our time. Badassery womanhood at its best!"—**Sara Gruen,** #1 *New York Times* bestselling author of *Water for Elephants*

"Fierce, beautiful and inspirational, Kim Michele Richardson has created a powerful tale about brave extraordinary heroines who are downright haunting and unforgettable." —**Abbott Kahler,** *New York Times* **bestselling author (as Karen Abbott) of** *The Ghosts of Eden Park*

ABOUT THE AUTHOR: *New York Times* and *USA Today* bestselling author, **Kim Michele Richardson,** is a multiple-award winning author who has written five works of historical fiction, and a bestselling memoir.

May 2022 | Hardcover | $26.99 | 9781728252995 | Sourcebooks
May 2022 | Paperback | $16.99 | 9781728242590 | Sourcebooks

CONVERSATION STARTERS

1. Discuss the types of circumstances in which a child, or parent, would ask for a Declaration of Emancipation. Thinking about Emancipation and the LeeAnn Rimes/Britney Spears issues where the child is earning huge dollars that the parent "manager" is squandering or keeping from the child improperly, what should be put in place to prevent this?

2. Children, especially rural children, were a valuable commodity to families who needed farm labor without having to pay wages. Because society was until recently, very patriarchal, it was the father who could 'express' emancipation and consent to his child's emancipation. Discuss Patriarchal Laws and the role it played in women and children's rights and lives and perhaps continues to play.

3. Honey's interactions with a far more sophisticated Pearl show a glimpse into innocence and youth. Though Honey has been well-educated by Book Woman, Cussy, in writing, reading, and more, her isolated life has held her back in other ways. Her new friend, Pearl is far ahead of Honey with modern gadgets, young men, parties and drinking. Discuss their differences, the women's strengths and vulnerabilities and their adjustments to new environments.

4. Discuss the different jobs Honey, Pearl, Bonnie and Amara held. What were the dangers they faced? What are unusual jobs women hold today verses years ago?

5. Child marriages are a global problem which can lead to dangerous and devastating consequences. In America, the marriageable age is determined by states. Many still allow child marriages between the ages of 14 to 17 with parental or judicial consent. There are some cases where children have married at ages 12 and younger. What are the dangers of being a child bride or groom?

6. Choose a character from the novel and imagine what their future would hold.

7. How do you think Honey, Cussy and Jackson's lives will evolve two decades later? What relevant laws will change, if any?

CHASING THE BLACK EAGLE

Bruce Geddes

Against a backdrop of the Harlem Renaissance and Haile Selassie's Ethiopia, a young man tails Hubert Julian—a pilot, inventor, adventurer, charlatan, and possible threat to America.

Facing an attempted murder charge, seventeen-year-old Arthur Tormes is in no position to refuse when a federal agent named Riley Triggs offers him a deal: all charges get dropped and Arthur goes free if he agrees to help the Bureau with a problem.

That problem is Hubert Julian, a.k.a. the Black Eagle of Harlem: inventor, pilot, parachutist, daredevil, charlatan, and one of the most extraordinary and popular figures of the Harlem Renaissance. For Triggs, it's the popularity that makes Julian a serious threat to the well-being of America.

To win his freedom, Arthur begins a spying mission that will occupy the next thirteen years of his life, taking him from 1920s New York City to Ethiopia on the verge of war—often at great personal cost. In the end, while America remains safe, Arthur Tormes's fate is less certain.

"Brucc Gcddcs is a master storyteller with an incredible ability to take us to dizzying heights, be it on the wings of the Black Eagle taking flight or to harrowing truths found in the underbelly of racism, anti-colonial fights, betrayal, including the worst of all, when one goes against themselves. A thoroughly enjoyable encounter of friendship, survival and above all, the human spirit." —**Chidiqgo Akunyili-Parr, author of** *I Am Because We Are*

"A novel that juggles genres—spy, noir, coming-of-age, romance—with charm, wit and seemingly effortless grace."—**Spencer Gordon, author of** *Cosmo*

ABOUT THE AUTHOR: **Bruce Geddes** is the author of one previous novel, *The Higher the Monkey Climbs*. His short fiction has appeared in the *New Quarterly*, *Blank Spaces Magazine*, and the *Freshwater Review*. Born in Windsor, Ontario, he currently lives in Kingston, Canada.

May 2023 | Paperback | $19.99 | 9781459750593 | Dundurn Press

CONVERSATION STARTERS

1. Is Hubert Julian a hero? Or a scoundrel?

2. Are Arthur Tormes and Hubert Julian friends? Are Arthur and Sergio Pratti friends?

3. Arthur has plenty of opportunities to escape the grip of Riley Triggs. Why doesn't he flee?

4. Discuss the role of freedom in the novel.

5. Jean Fox tries to explain her party-girl behaviour as part of a search for something. She never really defines it. What do you think she was looking for? How does that search relate to her parents' deaths?

6. Hubert Julian had an up-and-down relationship with the press. Sometimes they loved him, sometimes they hated him, sometimes they ridiculed him. How does the celebrity culture in the novel compare to our own era?

7. How would Hubert Julian's life be different if he'd been white?

8. While under Triggs' control, Arthur's behaviour has significant collateral damage to people he cares about. How much of the blame lies with him?

9. Discuss the role of responsibility in this novel.

COCOON

Zhang Yueran, Jeremy Tiang (Translator)

Cheng Gong and Li Jiaqi go way back. Both hailing from dysfunctional families, they grew up together in a Chinese provincial capital in the 1980s. Now, many years later, the childhood friends reunite and discover how much they still have in common. Both have always been determined to follow the tracks of their grandparents' generation to the heart of a mystery that perhaps should have stayed buried. What exactly happened during that rainy night in 1967, in the abandoned water tower? Zhang Yueran's layered and hypnotic prose reveals much about the unshakable power of friendship and the existence of hope. Hers is a unique fresh voice representing a new generation of important young writers from China, shedding a different light on the country's recent past.

"Cocoon is a stupendous novel, a beautiful and formidable achievement on the grandest scale. Its ruthless psychological realism is wondrously amplified by Zhang Yueran's magical powers of description. Zhang Yueran's scenes and images have an unworldly gleam of both hard-won insight and timeless truth. The novel is a triumph." —**Ian McEwan, author of the international Bestseller** *Atonement*

"Zhang dazzles with an intricately crafted web of secrets centered on two childhood friends in China. In lyrical prose, Zhang deeply humanizes her leads as they look to the past in an effort to understand themselves. It adds up to a remarkable and tragic story of family and community." —*Publishers Weekly,* **Starred Review**

ABOUT THE AUTHOR: **Zhang Yueran** is one of China's most influential young writers. Her novel *Cocoon* sold more than 120,000 copies in China and has been translated into several languages. In France it was nominated for the Best Foreign Book Prize 2019 and won the Best Asian Novel of the Prix Transfuge 2019. Zhang has been chief editor of *Newwriting* since 2008 and teaches literature and creative writing at Renmin University in China.

October 2022 | Paperback | $19.99 | 9781642861051 | World Editions

CONVERSATION STARTERS

1. What do you think are the main themes of the novel? Which stood out most to you, and why?

2. Did you feel like you learned much about the political history of China from this work? Would you be interested to learn more?

3. Zhang Yueran is a very popular author in her homeland. How do you think this work was received in China itself?

4. What do you think is the significance of the title, *Cocoon*? In France, the book is called Le Clou, or "The Nail." How do you think this shifts the emphasis, and do you think that's a good thing or not?

5. How would you describe the relationship between the two main characters in the story? What do you think they might have done differently in order not to become estranged from each other?

6. There are many other relationships within this novel, such as that of Li Jiaqi's father and Wang Luhan; Jiaqi's father and Luhan's mother; Jiaqi's mother and Li Jisheng; Cheng Gong's auntie and grandma—which of these interested you the most and why? Where there any interpersonal relationships you would have liked to have been explored more in this novel?

7. What do you imagine for Peixuan's future? What did you think of her character in general? Did any of your sympathies lie with her?

8. What did you make of Li Jiaqi's occasional destructive behavior, her attitude towards her lovers, and her inability to get over her father's death? What do you see for her in the future?

9. Some characters feel like happiness can be betrayal. This comes up in Jiaqi's relationship with Yachen, and Luhan's mother is said to feel this way. What situations give rise to this sentiment?

10. People in *Cocoon* seem to be defined, sometimes even to choose to be defined, by their personal or national history. What does the novel say about fate? On the other hand, there are characters who seem to choose to ignore reality in order to find happiness. Are they ever shown to be anything but naive or even shallow?

11. Is it Jaiqi's obsession with the impact of history and family that makes it inescapable for her, as one of her boyfriends suggests? Or is it the other way around?

CRADLES OF THE REICH

Jennifer Coburn

Through thorough research and with deep empathy, this chilling historical novel goes inside one of the Lebensborn Society maternity homes that existed in several countries during World War II, where thousands of "racially fit" babies were bred and taken from their mothers to be raised as part of the new Germany.

At the Heim Hochland maternity home in Bavaria, three women's lives coverage as they find themselves there under very different circumstances. Gundi is a pregnant university student from Berlin. An Aryan beauty, she's secretly a member of a resistance group. Hilde, only eighteen, is a true believer in the cause and is thrilled to carry a Nazi official's child. And Irma, a 44-year-old nurse, is desperate to build a new life for herself after personal devastation. Despite their opposing beliefs, all three have everything to lose as they begin to realize they are trapped within Hitler's terrifying scheme to build a Nazi-Aryan nation.

A cautionary tale for modern times told in stunning detail, *Cradles of the Reich* uncovers a little-known Nazi atrocity but also carries an uplifting reminder of the power of women to set aside differences and work together in solidarity in the face of oppression.

"*Every historical fiction novel should strive to be this compelling, well-researched and just flat-out good.*" —**Associated Press**

"*Skillfully researched and told with great care and insight, here is a World War II story whose lessons should not-must not-be forgotten.*" — **Susan Meissner, bestselling author of** *The Nature of Fragile Things*

"*A deep well of discussion topics for book-club readers.*" —*Kirkus Reviews*

ABOUT THE AUTHOR: **Jennifer Coburn** is a *USA Today* bestselling author of six novels and contributor to four literary anthologies. Over the past two decades, Coburn has received numerous awards from the Press Club and Society for Professional Journalists.

July 2023 | Paperback | $16.99 | 9781728269832 | Sourcebooks

CONVERSATION STARTERS

1. Gundi, Hilde, and Irma have starkly different attitudes toward the Nazi regime and their places at Heim Hochland. Who did you most identify with? Who did you find most compelling as a character?

2. Compare Hilde's and Gundi's experiences during the November pogroms the Nazis called Kristallnacht. Did either of them really understand the broader context of this event?

3. As Hilde tries to impress Nazi officials, she represses her conscience to say the right things. What motivates her to seek status within the Reich? What does Hilde want out of life?

4. How did the Reich's propaganda about self-sacrifice smooth the way for Lebensborn homes to function?

5. There are many examples of the Reich's coordinated effort to dehumanize Jews, from the picture book about poisonous mushrooms to the documentary The Eternal Jew. How do these materials relate to Lotte's insistence that "great things only happen when strong people make difficult choices"?

6. Put yourself in Gundi's shoes when she learns that the father of her child has been framed for a crime and sent to a labor camp. Would you be able to keep your secret? Would you look for a way to help Leo?

7. While the book focuses primarily on birth mothers, adoptive parents are an enormous part of the machinery of the Lebensborn Society. What circumstances led Germans to become adoptive parents? How, as in the case of the "displaced" Polish orphans, does adoption contribute to genocide?

8. How does Gundi's self-image get in the way of her first attempts to find Leo and get to know him?

9. Gundi's escape from Heim Hochland almost fails several times. Which close call made you the most nervous?

10. Irma says she doesn't want to live in a world where helping people survive is remarkable. How can we make that more ordinary in the modern day?

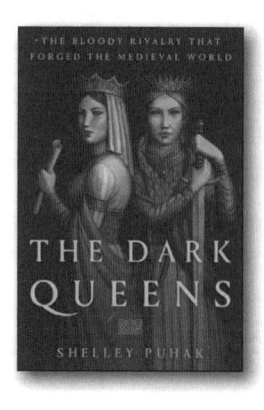

THE DARK QUEENS

Shelley Puhak

The Bloody Rivalry That Forged the Medieval World

The remarkable, little-known story of two trailblazing women in the Early Middle Ages who wielded immense power, only to be vilified for daring to rule.

Brunhild was a princess, raised to be married off for alliance-building. Her sister-in-law Fredegund started out as a palace slave. And yet—in sixth-century Merovingian France, where women were excluded from noble succession and royal politics, these two strategists reigned over vast realms.

They commanded armies and negotiated with kings, formed coalitions and broke them, mothered children and lost them. They fought a decades-long civil war—against each other. With ingenuity, they battled to stay alive in the game of statecraft, and in the process laid the foundations of what would one day be Charlemagne's empire. Yet after the queens' deaths, their stories were rewritten, their names consigned to legend.

In *The Dark Queens*, Shelley Puhak sets the record straight. She resurrects two women in all their complexity, painting a portrait of an unfamiliar time and striking at the roots of some of our culture's stubbornest myths about female power.

"*Medieval history at its most fun.* Game of Thrones, *eat your heart out!*"
—*Napa Valley Register*

"*A well-researched and well-told epic history.* The Dark Queens *brings these courageous, flawed, and ruthless rulers and their distant times back to life.*"
—**Margot Lee Shetterly**, *New York Times* **bestselling author of** *Hidden Figures*

ABOUT THE AUTHOR: **Shelley Puhak** is a critically acclaimed poet and writer whose work has appeared in the *Atlantic, Lapham's Quarterly, Teen Vogue, Virginia Quarterly Review*, and elsewhere. Her essays have been included in *The Best American Travel Writing* and selected as Notables in four consecutive editions of *The Best American Essays*. She is the author of two books of poetry, most recently *Guinevere in Baltimore*, winner of the Anthony Hecht Prize. *The Dark Queens* is her nonfiction debut. She lives in Maryland.

April 2023 | Paperback | $19.99 | 9781639730759 | Bloomsbury Publishing

CONVERSATION STARTERS

1. Why does Puhak call Brunhild and Fredegund the Dark Queens?

2. What can the erasure of the queens tell us about how history is written?

3. Look at the endnotes for chapter 1. How did Puhak use inference to shape the scene of Brunhild and Sigibert's wedding? What do those details add?

4. In Francia, 561, the Merovingians were poised for conflict. Why?

5. Who was Brunhild? Why did she find herself in Metz?

6. Fredegund's introduction is indirect, with her name mentioned occasionally before chapter 6. What is the effect of this trickle of information before a full introduction?

7. Chapter 5 ends with Galswintha's death and Chilperic's hasty marriage to Fredegund. Puhak describes her as "arrayed in the brightly dyed linens and jewels of her predecessor . . . smiling up at Chilperic." What does this description tell us about Fredegund?

8. Throughout the book, Brunhild and Fredegund would find themselves at odds with each other. What are some reasons for why they may not like each other?

9. What were some of the ways that both queens held on to power? Were they successful?

10. The question of an heir was a focus in both queens' lives. Why was it so important for both women to have a son? What was at stake for both women?

11. Fredegund was known to have ordered assassinations of her rivals for power. Compare that to her military talents later in the book. What does this tell us about Fredegund?

12. Talk about some of the Merovingian princesses in the book. What kind of power and agencies did they have?

13. What were some of the ways that society tried to control women during the time? How did both women subvert these?

14. Fredegund and Brunhild died in very different ways. How did each death make us feel?

DR. NO

Percival Everett

The protagonist of Percival Everett's puckish new novel is a brilliant professor of mathematics who goes by Wala Kitu. (Wala, he explains, means "nothing" in Tagalog, and Kitu is Swahili for "nothing.") He is an expert on nothing. That is to say, he is an expert, and his area of study is nothing, and he does nothing about it. This makes him the perfect partner for the aspiring villain John Sill, who wants to break into Fort Knox to steal, well, not gold bars but a shoebox containing nothing. Once he controls nothing he'll proceed with a dastardly plan to turn a Massachusetts town into nothing. Or so he thinks.

With the help of the brainy and brainwashed astrophysicist-turned-henchwoman Eigen Vector, our professor tries to foil the villain while remaining in his employ. In the process, Wala Kitu learns that Sill's desire to become a literal Bond villain originated in some real all-American villainy related to the murder of Martin Luther King Jr. As Sill says, "Professor, think of it this way. This country has never given anything to us and it never will. We have given everything to it. I think it's time we gave nothing back."

Dr. No is a caper with teeth, a wildly mischievous novel from one of our most inventive, provocative, and productive writers. That it is about nothing isn't to say that it's not about anything. In fact, it's about villains. Bond villains. And that's not nothing.

"Immensely enjoyable. . . . Throughout, Everett boldly makes a farce out of real-world nightmares, and the rapid-fire pacing leaves readers little time to blink. Satire doesn't get much sharper or funnier than this." —**Publishers Weekly**, **Starred Review**

"Everett continues to be an endlessly inventive, genre-devouring creator of thoughtful, tender, provocative, and absolutely unpredictable literary wonders." —**Booklist**, **Starred Review**

ABOUT THE AUTHOR: **Percival Everett** is the author of more than thirty books, most recently *The Trees* and *Telephone*.

November 2022 | Paperback | $16.00 | 9781644452080 | Graywolf Press

CONVERSATION STARTERS

1. How does *Dr. No* play with and complicate the idea of villainy?

2. How is *Dr. No* similar to other mystery/spy/thriller plots you've encountered? How is it different?

3. On page 59, Wala Kitu says, "I admitted to myself, once again, that I was, if not stupid, at least profoundly adrift, astray." Is Kitu actually a genius? A fool? Is there a difference? Does it matter?

4. John Sill and his family are connected to crime as both perpetrators and victims. How do these crimes affect his actions?

5. Give some examples of how *Dr. No* is simultaneously humorous and serious. Could one aspect work without the other?

6. What part does race play in the novel? Additionally, what part does wealth play? Are these two linked, and if so, how?

7. How does Kitu's one-legged dog, Trigo, influence the narrative? Does he possess extraordinary communicative powers, or is Kitu truly dreaming?

8. Is *Dr. No* really a math novel disguised as a genre novel? Which was your favorite logic puzzle or math reference? How do these elements affect the experience of reading the novel?

9. We're almost to the last question, and we still haven't talked about nothing—which is obviously the animating force behind this whole novel. How does Everett use nothing to create a powerful effect in the novel—as a character, a concept, a joke, an existential threat?

10. With that in mind, did you find nothing changed by your reading of *Dr. No*?

11. And furthermore, in the end, is all fiction really just nothing?

DUST CHILD
Nguyễn Phan Quế Mai

From the bestselling author of *The Mountains Sing*, a richly poetic and suspenseful saga about two Vietnamese sisters, an American veteran, and an Amerasian man whose lives intersect in surprising ways, set during and after the war in Việt Nam.

In 1969, sisters Trang and Quỳnh, desperate to help their parents pay off debts, leave their rural village to work at a bar in Sài Gòn. Once in the big city, the young girls are thrown headfirst into a world they were not expecting.

Decades later, past and present converge as the characters come together to confront decisions made during a time of war—decisions that reverberate throughout one another's lives and ultimately allow them to find common ground across race, generation, culture, and language. Immersive, moving, and lyrical, *Dust Child* tells an unforgettable story of how those who inherited tragedy can redefine their destinies with hard-won wisdom, compassion, courage, and joy.

Named a Best Book of March/Spring 2023 by the *Los Angeles Times*, *Cosmo*, *Reader's Digest*, GMA.com, *Ms. Magazine*, Amazon, the *Chicago Review of Books*, BookPage, and BookBub.

"Nguyễn Phan Quế Mai will win many more readers with her powerful and deeply empathetic second novel. Dust Child *establishes Nguyen Phan Que Mai as one of our finest observers of the devastating consequences of war."*
—*Booklist*, **Starred Review**

ABOUT THE AUTHOR: Born and raised in Việt Nam, **Nguyễn Phan Quế Mai** is the author of *The Mountains Sing*, winner of the 2020 BookBrowse Best Debut Award, the 2021 International Book Awards, the 2021 PEN Oakland/Josephine Miles Literary Award, and the 2020 Lannan Literary Award Fellowship for Fiction. Her writing has been translated into twenty languages and has appeared in major publications, including the *New York Times*. She has a PhD in creative writing from Lancaster University. She is an advocate for the rights of disadvantaged groups in Việt Nam and has founded several scholarship programs, and she was named by Forbes Vietnam as one of twenty inspiring women of 2021. For more information, visit: http://www.nguyenphanquemai.com.

March 2023 | Hardcover | $ 28.00 | 9781643752754 | Algonquin Books

CONVERSATION STARTERS

1. What did you know about the struggles of Amerasians born into the Việt Nam War before you read this book? How do Phong's experiences influence your thoughts about the impact of wars? What could be done to prevent these struggles?

2. Does the author subvert or challenge the persistent Western trope of a passive Asian woman abandoned by her lover (think Madame Butterfly and Miss Saigon)? In what ways do Trang and Quỳnh refuse to be seen only be as victims?

3. Asian women in Hollywood films and Việt Nam War literature, if included at all, are often portrayed one-dimensionally as prostitutes, there to either exploit or service or to comfort American soldiers. How do Trang and Quỳnh challenge and break those stereotypes?

4. Describe Dan when he first arrived in Việt Nam in 1969. Why is Trang first attracted to him? Trace how—and how much—the war changes Dan. Can wars have the power to erode the characters of human beings? Give examples of other stories that illustrate this.

5. What are the root causes of Dan's trauma? When Dan returns to Việt Nam he seems only concerned with trying to deal with his PTSD. How do his interactions with the Vietnamese he meets shift that self-centered concern to a search for what Linda calls "atonement"?

6. Via the experiences of Linda and Thanh (the son of the Northern Vietnamese veteran who suffers from Alzheimer's), describe how war trauma is inherited by family members? What have Linda and Thanh done to help their loved ones cope with their trauma?

7. "You American vets have benefits, paid by your government. We have nothing. You have a wall in Washington, but we aren't acknowledged there. We fought for you, alongside you, yet you pretend we don't exist." Thiên told Dan in the novel. What are the causes of Thiên's resentment and are they justified?

8. Why do some mothers of Amerasians not want to be found? Why do some American veterans refuse to acknowledge their Amerasian children when they are located? Discuss the ethics and complexity involved in Amerasians' search for missing family members. Are these ethical issues similar to a general search for family members?

THE FAMILY CHAO

Lan Samantha Chang

Barack Obama's 2022 Summer Reading List

A *Vogue* Best Book of the Year

A Literary Hub Most Anticipated Book of 2022

The residents of Haven, Wisconsin, have dined on the Fine Chao restaurant's delicious Americanized Chinese food for thirty-five years, content to ignore any unsavory whispers about the family owners. Whether or not Big Leo Chao is honest, or his wife, Winnie, is happy, their food tastes good and their three sons earned scholarships to respectable colleges. But when the brothers reunite in Haven, the Chao family's secrets and simmering resentments erupt at last.

Before long, brash, charismatic, and tyrannical patriarch Leo is found dead—presumed murdered—and his sons find they've drawn the exacting gaze of the entire town. The ensuing trial brings to light potential motives for all three brothers: Dagou, the restaurant's reckless head chef; Ming, financially successful but personally tortured; and the youngest, gentle but lost college student James. As the spotlight on the brothers tightens—and the family dog meets an unexpected fate—Dagou, Ming, and James must reckon with the legacy of their father's outsized appetites and their own future survival.

Brimming with heartbreak, comedy, and suspense, *The Family Chao* offers a kaleidoscopic, highly entertaining portrait of a Chinese American family grappling with the dark undercurrents of a seemingly pleasant small town.

"A riveting character-driven novel." —**Ilana Masad**, *NPR*

"A hilarious mystery that's also a searing take on assimilation and the American dream." —**People Magazine**

ABOUT THE AUTHOR: **Lan Samantha Chang** is the author of three novels: *The Family Chao*, *Inheritance*, and *All Is Forgotten, Nothing Is Lost*. The director of the Iowa Writers' Workshop, she lives in Iowa City.

November 2022 | Paperback | $16.95 | 9781324050469 | W. W. Norton & Co.

CONVERSATION STARTERS

1. Lan Samantha Chang's *The Family Chao* is rife with lost possessions: Alf, the blue carpetbag, and the jade ring, to name a few. What else was lost? How do these lost items progress the plot? What is their symbolic function?

2. Why is Katherine's appetite for Chinese food full of "complications" that are "played out in the real world, not in her palate"? (81) How does this compare to Ming's rejection of Chinese food? What does this suggest about the relationship between food and belonging? Are there any foods or meals in your life that help you perform particular identities?

3. *The Family Chao* is divided into two parts: "They See Themselves" and "The World Sees Them." How do these sections differ in terms of tone, narrative voice, and subject? Who is "the world"? Who are "they"? How do both interrelate? What does this distinction imply about your presence as a reader?

4. To what extent does the aphorism "Like man, like dog" (61) capture the novel's exploration of desire? How do dogs appear throughout the novel, and what might this motif signify?

5. How does the idea of sacrifice resonate throughout *The Family Chao*? What does each character sacrifice? For whom? With what intentions? In what social, political, and economic contexts? How do your experiences shape your emotional connection to each character's struggles?

6. Ming tells James that "America is not a democracy, it's not a place of opportunity . . . if you can't choose to be white" (94). How does *The Family Chao*'s narrative uphold this statement?

7. From her hospital bed, Winnie asks Dagou, "If you don't love your father, how can you begin to love the world?" (111) How does this interaction explore themes of familial duty and loyalty? How do protagonists define themselves through family? How do different characters' understandings of love shift throughout the novel? In what way does your experience of love influence your reading?

ReadingGroupChoices.com

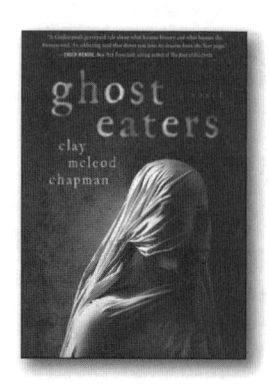

GHOST EATERS

Clay McLeod Chapman

A Library Reads Pick

An Indie Next Pick

This terrifying supernatural page-turner will make you think twice about opening doors to the unknown.

Erin hasn't been able to set a single boundary with her charismatic but reckless college ex-boyfriend, Silas. When he asks her to bail him out of rehab—again—she knows she needs to cut him off. But days after he gets out, Silas turns up dead of an overdose in their hometown of Richmond, Virginia, and Erin's world falls apart.

Then a friend tells her about Ghost, a new drug that allows users to see the dead. Wanna get haunted? he asks. Grieving and desperate for closure with Silas, Erin agrees to a pill-popping "séance." But the drug has unfathomable side effects—and once you take it, you can never go back.

"Shades of *Flatliners* and addiction drama pepper this tale about a woman who learns her college sweetheart died of an overdose—from a drug that allows folks to see the dead." —*USA Today*

"A legitimately terrifying ghost story and also a thoughtful and smart (if grim) exploration of how addiction destroys lives, *Ghost Eaters* should make Clay McLeod Chapman a star." —*Vulture*

"A great choice for fans of *A Head Full of Ghosts* by Paul Tremblay, *Mexican Gothic* by Silvia Moreno-Garcia, and *Orphans of Bliss*, edited by Mark Matthews."—*Booklist*, **starred review**

"A high anxiety, utterly original, and compelling contemplation of what it means to be haunted."—*Library Journal*

"A terrifying meditation of the horrors of modern life and our collective fixation with death."—*Library Journal*

ABOUT THE AUTHOR: **Clay McLeod Chapman** writes novels, comic books, and children's books, as well as for film and TV. He is the author of the horror novels *The Remaking* and *Whisper Down the Lane*.

September 2022 | Hardcover | $21.99 | 9781683692171 | Quirk Books
June 2023 | Paperback | $16.99 | 9781683693789 | Quirk Books

CONVERSATION STARTERS

1. At the beginning of the book, readers are introduced to college friends Silas, Erin, Amara, and Tobias in a cemetery. What were your first impressions of the group? And how does it foreshadow future events?

2. After losing Silas to an overdose, Erin is dealing with booth guilt and grief. Which emotion do you think drives her to take a drug like Ghost?

3. The pill-popping séance that Erin, Amara, and Tobias have occurs in an unfinished and abandoned housing development. Why do you think the author chose this setting?

4. Erin experiences unfathomable side effects under the influence of ghost. Which side effect stuck with the you the most? And why do you think she kept going back for more?

5. Would you take a pill like Ghost for the opportunity to be reunited with a loved one?

6. The aftermath of addiction is horrifying. Did you find how addiction is depicted in this book relatable?

7. How do you think the use of the supernatural captured the real life horrors of addiction and America's sordid history?

8. What do you imagine happens to Erin after the book ends?

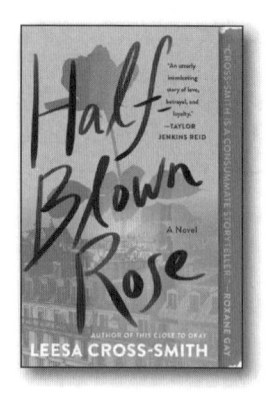

HALF-BLOWN ROSE

Leesa Cross-Smith

An irresistible story of a woman remaking her life after her husband's betrayal leads to a year of travel, art, and passion in Paris, from the award-winning author of *This Close to Okay*.

Vincent, having grown up as the privileged daughter of artists, has a lovely life in many ways. At forty-four, she enjoys strolling the streets of Paris and teaching at the modern art museum; she has a vibrant group of friends; and she's even caught the eye of a young, charismatic man named Loup. But Vincent is also in Paris to escape a painful betrayal: her husband, Cillian, has published a bestselling book divulging secrets about their marriage and his own past, hinting that he may have abandoned a young woman and their child back in Dublin before he moved to California and never returned.

Now estranged, Vincent has agreed to see Cillian again at their son's upcoming wedding, but Loup introduces new complications. Soon they begin an intense affair, and somewhere between dinners made together, cigarettes smoked in the moonlight, hazy evenings in nightclubs, and long, starry walks along the Seine, Vincent feels herself loosening and blossoming.

In a journey that is both transportive and intimate, *Half-Blown Rose* traverses Paris, art, travel, liminal spaces, and the messy complexities of relationships and romance, with excerpts from Cillian's novel, playlists, and journal entries woven throughout. As Cillian does all he can to win her back, Vincent must decide what she wants . . . and who she will be.

"An utterly intoxicating story of love, betrayal, and loyalty." —**Taylor Jenkins Reid**, *New York Times* bestselling author of *Malibu Rising*

ABOUT THE AUTHOR: **Leesa Cross-Smith** is a homemaker and the author of *Every Kiss A War*, *Whiskey & Ribbons*, *So We Can Glow*, and *This Close to Okay*. She lives in Kentucky with her husband and their two teenagers.

April 2023 | Paperback | $17.99 | 9781538755181 | Grand Central Publishing

CONVERSATION STARTERS

1. What are some of the different ways in which we find and define ourselves? How does Vincent? Does this change at all throughout the novel?

2. There are many descriptions of food throughout *Half-Blown Rose*, from Vincent and Loup's eating fruit in her kitchen, to indulgent dinner parties, and more. Discuss what significance or symbolism different foods might have in the story.

3. Compare and contrast Vincent's relationships with Cillian and Loup. What does she get from each relationship? Is she able to access different parts of herself when she's with them? When she's alone?

4. What kinds of family structures and types of romantic relationships do you see in this novel? Was your reaction to Vincent's choices or the relationship dynamics in the book ever informed by predominant social/societal norms?

5. What are some examples of actions or gestures that Vincent, Cillian, and Loup make to convey their emotions to their loved ones? Are there instances in which you think a gesture is insufficient to communicate feelings?

6. How do you think being in Paris affects Vincent's emotional journey after Cillian's betrayal?

7. Examine Cillian's novel excerpts and Vincent's journal entries. How do they inform the novel as a whole? What can you tell about them and the way they each perceive the world based on their writing?

8. In Vincent's travel journal, she considers the liminal nature of travel and certain spaces surrounding it, like airports. Discuss liminal spaces in the book and why they might resonate with Vincent. Are you drawn to any liminal spaces in your own life?

9. If you were Vincent, would you be able to forgive Cillian? And would you go back to him?

10. Vincent notes to Loup: "I've read this book before, by the way…what we're doing…I know how it ends. If a man were writing this story I'd have to die, right? You've read *Anna Karenina…Madame Bovary*?" (173). What does she mean? How does *Half-Blown Rose* play on or subvert classic literary themes surrounding women and sex?

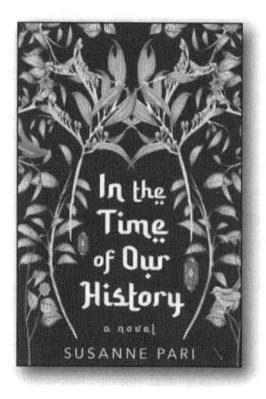

IN THE TIME OF OUR HISTORY

Susanne Pari

Inspired by her own family's experiences as exiles in America following the 1979 Islamic Revolution, Susanne Pari explores the tensions between tradition and identity, duty and desire, exile and home, as the prodigal daughter of Iranian immigrants returns to her family's home to honor the One Year anniversary of her sister's tragic death in late 1990s New Jersey.

It is 1998 when Mitra Jahani reluctantly returns to her New Jersey hometown for her sister's "One Year." This Persian custom of marking the anniversary of a person's death is one of many traditions and beliefs against which Mitra, the American-born daughter of Iranian immigrants, has spent her life rebelling. But her trepidation goes beyond this culture clash and her own overwhelming grief over the loss of her sister.

Even as Mitra dreads sharing space with the domineering father who banished her for refusing a traditional path, her mother hopes for a chance at reconciliation. Shireen has walked a fine line all these years between her fierce love for her surviving daughter and her loyalty to her husband. Yet his callousness even amid shattering loss has compelled her to rethink her own decades of submission. And when Mitra is suddenly forced to confront hard truths about her sister's life, and the secrets each of them hid to protect others, mother and daughter reach a new understanding—and forge an unexpected path forward.

"Beautifully written. . . I'm still thinking about the women who inhabited these pages, the choices they made, and the love between them."—**Lisa See**, *New York Times* bestselling author of *The Island of Sea Women*

"I fell in love with this jewel of a novel from the first page." —**Amy Tan**, *New York Times* bestselling author of *The Joy Luck Club*

ABOUT THE AUTHOR: **Susanne Pari** is an Iranian-American novelist and journalist who lived in both the United States and Iran until the 1979 Islamic Revolution forced her family into permanent exile. She now divides her time between Northern California and New York and can be found online at SusannePari.com.

January 2023 | Paperback | $16.99 | 9781496739261 | Kensington Books

CONVERSATION STARTERS

1. *In the Time of Our History* tells the story of a secular and educated immigrant family, most of whose members have resettled in the United States because of a Revolution that gave rise to a brutal regime in Iran. Can you imagine yourself in a similar situation? How do you think you would cope with exile and migration to a foreign country? Many of the Jahanis cling to old traditions in order to retain a sense of belonging. Which beliefs and norms would you try to preserve?

2. Mitra and Anahita are first generation Americans, while the rest of the Jahanis are immigrants. What are some of the ways the sisters are different from the others? Do you think the presence of the extended family in their lives influenced their personalities and choices?

3. Revelation and growth is a theme for many of this novel's characters. Could you relate to Shireen's journey away from stalwart wife toward independent woman? If Anahita and the children hadn't died, do you think Shireen would have taken this path?

4. The romance between Mitra and Julian is complex. While their devotion to each other may run deep, there are obstacles that stand in the way of a future for them together. Do you think these obstacles could have been overcome?

5. Both Salimeh and Zoya are refugees. How are they similar? How are they different? If they wound up on your doorstep, would you help one or both or neither?

6. Yusef is depicted mostly as a ruthless and narcissistic patriarch, not to mention a cold and unfaithful husband. And yet, he also has a traumatic history. Did this history of trauma excuse any of his behavior? And does he achieve some redemption in your mind in the end?

7. Autocracies survive when they can control the substance and flow of information to their citizens. This requires a ruthless vigilance to silence intellectuals and creatives. Have you ever been in a situation where you were afraid of writing or saying something you believed?

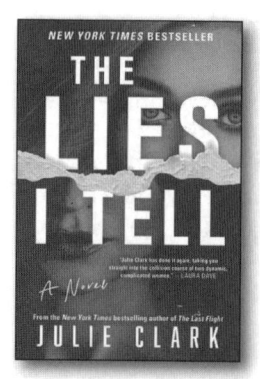

THE LIES I TELL

Julie Clark

THE INSTANT *NEW YORK TIMES* BESTSELLER

BOOK OF THE MONTH SELECTION

BUZZFEED'S MOST ANTICIPATED THILLERS OF 2022

POPSUGAR'S MOST ANTICIPATED THRILLERS OF 2022

From the *New York Times* bestselling author of *The Last Flight* comes a twisted con-woman thriller about two women out for revenge—or is it justice?

Meg Williams. Maggie Littleton. Melody Wilde. Different names for the same person, depending on the town, depending on the job. She's a con artist who erases herself to become whoever you need her to be—a college student. A life coach. A real estate agent. Nothing about her is real. She slides alongside you and tells you exactly what you need to hear, and by the time she's done, you've likely lost everything.

Kat Roberts has been waiting ten years for the woman who upended her life to return. And now that she has, Kat is determined to be the one to expose her. But as the two women grow closer, Kat's long-held assumptions begin to crumble, leaving Kat to wonder who Meg's true target is.

"Riveting." —**Laura Dave**, *New York Times* bestselling author of *The Last Thing He Told Me*

"A meticulously plotted mindbender. Do not miss it." —**Jessica Knoll**, *New York Times* bestselling author of *Luckiest Girl Alive*

"Smart, savvy and so duplicitous with a propulsive storyline... Julie Clark does it again!" —**Mary Kubica**, *New York Times* bestselling author of *Local Woman Missing*

ABOUT THE AUTHOR: **Julie Clark** is the *New York Times* bestselling author of *The Lies I Tell* and *The Last Flight*, both of which were also #1 international bestsellers and have been translated into more than twenty-five languages. She lives in Los Angeles with her family and a goldendoodle.

January 2023 | Paperback | $16.99 | 9781496739261 | Kensington Books

CONVERSATION STARTERS

1. One of the most powerful tools in Meg's arsenal is a familiarity with social media. What do you think she could learn about you from your online presence?

2. Since they both know the other woman is lying about her identity, Meg and Kat also know they shouldn't trust each other. How does their friendship grow despite this?

3. Discuss the role of ego in Meg's cons. How do her targets create openings for her with their own bad behavior?

4. At first, Kat blames Meg for what happened with Nate. When do you think she stopped feeling that way?

5. The greatest downside of Meg's career is the loneliness. Do you think she could have kept in touch with her friends when she started scamming Cory? How would you feel in her position moving cross-country every few years and not making any permanent connections?

6. Meg believes that scamming Phillip to return Celia's cottage was a turning point in her career. How was that job different from the others she had run?

7. Why does it take Kat so long to recognize that Scott has relapsed? Where would you draw the line between supporting a partner who is trying to overcome an addiction and protecting yourself?

8. Kat doesn't trust that Scott will be investigated by his colleagues. Is there incentive for police departments to investigate their officers and detectives? What motivations do they have to sweep corruption and violence under the rug?

9. Meg posits, "The difference between justice and revenge comes down to who's telling the story." What does she mean, and do you agree with her?

10. What's next for Kat and Meg? Do you think Kat will succeed in her new quest? Will Meg really retire from cons?

THE LOST GIRLS OF WILLOWBROOK

Ellen Marie Wiseman

Instant *New York Times* **Bestseller**

Girl, Interrupted meets *American Horror Story* in 1970s Staten Island, as the *New York Times* bestselling author of *The Orphan Collector* blends fact, fiction, and urban legend for a haunting story about a young woman mistakenly imprisoned at Willowbrook State School—the real state-run institution that Geraldo Rivera would later expose for its horrifying abuses.

Even though they're identical twins, Sage always knew her sister was a little different. They loved the same things and shared a deep understanding, but Rosemary—awake to every emotion, easily moved to joy or tears—seemed to need more protection from the world.

Six years after Rosemary's death from pneumonia, Sage, now sixteen, still misses her deeply. Their mother perished in a car crash, and Sage's stepfather, Alan, resents being burdened by a responsibility he never wanted. Yet despite living as near strangers in their Staten Island apartment, Sage is stunned to discover that Alan has kept a shocking secret: Rosemary didn't die. She was committed to Willowbrook State School and has lingered there until just a few days ago, when she went missing.

Sage knows little about Willowbrook. It's always been a place shrouded by rumor and mystery. A place local parents threaten to send misbehaving kids. With no idea what to expect, Sage secretly sets out for the institution, determined to find Rosemary. What she learns, once she steps through its doors and is mistakenly believed to be her sister, will change her life in ways she never could have imagined.

ABOUT THE AUTHOR: **Ellen Marie Wiseman** is a *New York Times* bestselling author known for writing novels based on real historical injustices. Born and raised in Three Mile Bay, a tiny hamlet in northern New York, she is a first-generation German American who discovered her love of reading and writing while attending one of the last one-room schoolhouses in New York State. Visit her online at EllenMarieWiseman.com

August 2022 | Paperback | $16.95 | 9781496715883 | Kensington Books

CONVERSATION STARTERS

1. Located on Staten Island in New York from 1947-1987, Willowbrook State School was a state-run institution for children with disabilities that became known—tragically long before it was finally shut down—for its deplorable abuses. An estimated 12,000 residents died at Willowbrook due to neglect, violence and medical abuse. What was your awareness of Willowbrook before reading this novel? Why do you think most people today are unfamiliar with the history of Willowbrook?

2. In 1972, Geraldo Rivera's Peabody Award-winning exposé, "Willowbrook: The Last Great Disgrace," aired on national television, bringing widespread awareness of the institution's abuses. Shockingly, Willowbrook wouldn't be shut down for another 15 years. Were you surprised that Willowbrook was allowed to continue operating for so long? Why do you think it took decades to shut down the institution?

3. How would you react if, after grieving a loved one for years, you found out they were alive but had been committed to an institution like Willowbrook?

4. Willowbrook was grossly overcrowded, underfunded, and understaffed. While this novel negatively depicts most of the staff members, there were in reality many good, well-meaning people who worked at Willowbrook. There were also wonderful doctors who truly cared for the residents, such as Dr. Mike Wilkins and Dr. William Bronston, who risked their careers and more to improve conditions and bring justice to victims. Do you think the staff and doctors at Willowbrook were just as much victims of the institution as the residents? Why or why not? What do you think were the biggest factors that contributed to the horrible conditions and abuses at Willowbrook?

5. Sage remembers hearing rumors about scientific experiments being carried out on children at Willowbrook. This rumor turned out to be true. Did this surprise you? Have you ever heard of any other medical experiments being carried out in the U.S. on the disenfranchised, impoverished, orphaned, or ill?

6. *The Lost Girls of Willowbrook* was published on the 35th anniversary of Willowbrook's long overdue closure. Even though Willowbrook no longer exists, do you think the issues surrounding institutional abuse are still relevant today?

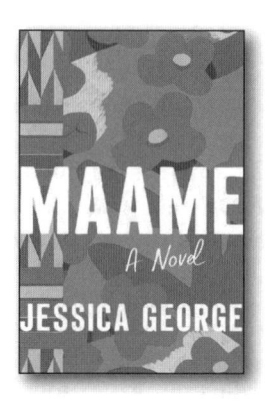

MAAME

Jessica George

A Read with Jenna, Today Show Book Club Pick and a *New York Times* Bestseller

Maame (ma-meh) has many meanings in Twi but in my case, it means woman.

It's fair to say that Maddie's life in London is far from rewarding. With a mother who spends most of her time in Ghana (yet still somehow manages to be overbearing), Maddie is the primary caretaker for her father, who suffers from advanced stage Parkinson's. At work, her boss is a nightmare and Maddie is tired of always being the only Black person in every meeting.

When her mum returns from her latest trip to Ghana, Maddie leaps at the chance to get out of the family home and finally start living. A self-acknowledged late bloomer, she's ready to experience some important "firsts": She finds a flat share, says yes to after-work drinks, pushes for more recognition in her career, and throws herself into the bewildering world of internet dating. But it's not long before tragedy strikes, forcing Maddie to face the true nature of her unconventional family, and the perils—and rewards—of putting her heart on the line.

Smart, funny, and deeply affecting, Jessica George's *Maame* deals with the themes of our time with humor and poignancy: from familial duty and racism, to female pleasure, the complexity of love, and the life-saving power of friendship. Most important, it explores what it feels like to be torn between two homes and cultures—and it celebrates finally being able to find where you belong.

"An utterly charming and deeply moving portrait of the joys—and the guilt—of trying to find your own way in life." —**Celeste Ng, #1** *New York Times* **bestselling author**

ABOUT THE AUTHOR: **Jessica George** was born and raised in London to Ghanaian parents and studied English Literature at the University of Sheffield. After working at a literary agency and a theatre, she landed a job in the editorial department of Bloomsbury UK. *Maame* is her first novel.

January 2023 | Hardcover | $27.99 | 9781250282521 | St Martin's Press

CONVERSATION STARTERS

1. How does the meaning of the word *Maame* evolve throughout the story, and how does Maddie's relationship to it change?

2. Google search results appear frequently throughout the novel. In what kind of situations does Maddie turn to Google for answers, and why do you think she does so? How did the inclusion of her search results affect your reading experience?

3. Maddie misses out on several social experiences because she is taking care of her father. How does this affect the way she views herself, particularly in relation to other young people her age?

4. How does religion and God play a role in this story? Are the two distinct at any points? Does their role in Maddie's life shift after her father passes away?

5. Maddie's mother tells her to "keep family matters private" (1). How does this affect Maddie's personal life and/or her ability to connect with people? How does this same directive affect how Maddie's mum lives her life?

6. At times, Maddie doesn't feel like she meets the expectations of her English environment or her Ghanaian culture. Have you or anyone you know struggled with a similar conflict?

7. Maddie is often the only Black person in the room at both of her jobs with CGT and OTP. This environment makes Maddie hyperaware of things like her hair or the food she eats. How does Maddie's race, gender, and culture affect her experience in the workplace? Compare and contrast Katherine's and Maddie's experiences in the workplace.

8. On page 14, Maddie explains that CGT hired her when they were focusing on "reflecting diversity." Months into the job, Maddie realized that the only other Black people she worked with "were mainly front of house, serving staff." What are your thoughts on this observation, and how companies in general treat diversity in the workplace? Do you notice any performative diversity in the story or in your own life?

9. To what extent does Maddie's relationship with her mother evolve over the course of the novel? What do you imagine for their dynamic in the future?

MOONRISE OVER NEW JESSUP

Jamila Minnicks

Winner of the 2021 PEN/Bellwether Prize for Socially Engaged Fiction, an enchanting and thought-provoking debut novel about a Black woman doing whatever it takes to protect all she loves on Alabama soil during the Civil Rights Movement.

It's 1957, and after leaving the only home she has ever known, Alice Young steps off the bus into all-Black New Jessup, where residents have largely rejected integration as the means for Black social advancement. Instead, they seek to maintain, and fortify, the community they cherish on their "side of the woods." In this place, Alice falls in love with Raymond Campbell, whose clandestine organizing activities challenge New Jessup's longstanding status quo and could lead to the young couple's expulsion—or worse—from the home they both hold dear. As they marry and raise children together, Alice must find a way to balance her undying support for his underground work with her desire to protect New Jessup from the rising pressure of upheaval from inside, and outside, their side of town.

Based on the history of the many Black towns and settlements established across the country, Jamila Minnicks's heartfelt and riveting debut is both a celebration of Black joy and a timely examination of the opposing viewpoints that attended desegregation in America.

"With compelling characters and a heart-pounding plot, Jamila Minnicks pulled me into pages of history I'd never turned before." —**Barbara Kingsolver**

"*Elegant and nuanced,* Moonrise Over New Jessup *is an incandescent work of art through-and-through, from a powerful new voice.*" —**Jason Mott, author of National Book Award winner** *Hell of a Book*

ABOUT THE AUTHOR: **Jamila Minnicks** is the author of *Moonrise Over New Jessup*, the 2021 winner of the PEN/Bellwether Prize for Socially Engaged Fiction. Her work is also published in *CRAFT Literary Magazine, The Write Launch,* and *The Silent World in Her Vase.* Her piece "Politics of Distraction" was nominated for a Pushcart Prize. She is a graduate of the University of Michigan, the Howard University School of Law, and Georgetown University. She lives in Washington, DC. Find her at www.jamila-minnicks.com.

January 2023 | Hardcover | $28.00 | 9781643752464 | Algonquin Books

CONVERSATION STARTERS

1. Why do you think Alice sobs when she first realizes that she's ended up in what appears to be a thriving, all-Black community? What did you think of the way she is embraced into the town by the Browns, Miss Vivian, and Mr. Marvin?

2. Though Alice, her friends, and family refer to New Jessup as a "town," it was never formally incorporated as a municipality after the 1903 riot. Technically, this would make it a Black settlement. Why do you think it was important to Raymond and the rest of the members of the New Jessup NNAS to incorporate New Jessup into its own city?

3. More often than not, the people of New Jessup say they are trying to maintain "separation" or "independence" from the other side of the woods, as opposed to saying "segregation" or "desegregation" or "integration". Why do you think this is? How do you think their language reflects their mindset about New Jessup?

4. White Citizens' Councils were organized in many localities after the Supreme Court issued the Brown v. Board of Education decision which desegregated public schools. These councils were generally created to fight desegregation and perpetuate anti-Black laws and conduct, and were generally comprised of "local white men of distinction" such as the judges, police, and business owners of Jessup. Why do you think they asked Pop, Cap, and Mr. Marvin to join their meetings? Why do you think Pop, Cap, and Mr. Marvin withheld information from the council and handled any organizing around New Jessup themselves?

5. Why do you believe that Raymond wanted Alice to stop working outside the home? And why do you think he ultimately forced the issue? What was your reaction when he had her fired?

6. Alice mentions wanting to vote, but that she is unwilling to "wear out her shoe leather" just to cast a ballot for the same candidates that are always on the ballot. Why do you think she took this position?

7. Why do you think Raymond considers the theft of his sister Regina's shoes the worst part of the altercation at the Montgomery bus station?

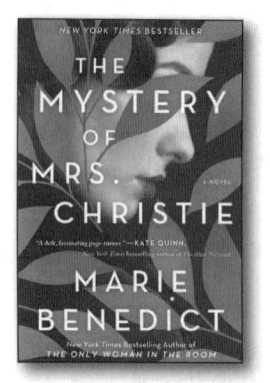

THE MYSTERY OF MRS. CHRISTIE

Marie Benedict

The instant *New York Times* and *USA Today* bestseller.

December 1926: England unleashes the largest manhunt in its history. The object of the search is not an escaped convict or a war criminal, but the missing wife of a WWI hero, up-and-coming mystery author Agatha Christie.

When her car is found wrecked, empty, and abandoned near a natural spring, the country is in a frenzy. Eleven days later, Agatha reappears, claiming amnesia. She provides no answers for her disappearance. That is...until she writes a very strange book about a missing woman, a murderous husband, and a plan to expose the truth.

The Mystery of Mrs. Christie explores a strong woman's successful endeavor to write her narrative and take her history into her own hands.

"Ingenious...it's possible that Benedict has brought to life the most plausible explanation for why Christie disappeared for 11 days in 1926."
—*The Washington Post*

"A whodunit infinitely worthy of its famous heroine. Benedict's exploration of Agatha Christie's life and mysterious disappearance will have book club discussions running overtime." —**Lisa Wingate**, **#1** *New York Times* **bestselling author of** *Before We Were Yours* **and** *The Book of Lost Friends*

"A deft, fascinating page-turner replete with richly drawn characters and plot twists that would stump Hercule Poirot." —**Kate Quinn**, *New York Times* **bestselling author of** *The Alice Network,* *The Huntress,* **and** *The Rose Code*

"Part domestic thriller, part Golden Age mystery—and all Marie Benedict!"
—**Lauren Willig**, *New York Times* **bestselling author**

ABOUT THE AUTHOR: **Marie Benedict** is an experienced litigator and magna cum laude graduate of Boston College and cum laude graduate of the Boston University School of Law. Marie, the author of many *New York Times* and *USA Today* bestsellers, views herself as an archaeologist of sorts, telling the untold stories of women. She lives in Pittsburgh with her family.

October 2021 | Paperback | $16.99 | 9781728234304 | Sourcebooks

CONVERSATION STARTERS

1. Agatha Christie is one of the most celebrated mystery writers of all time. What did you know about her personal history before you read *The Mystery of Mrs. Christie*? Did the book challenge any of your preconceived notions about her life?

2. Agatha Christie was a successful writer within her lifetime, quite unusual for a woman of her time. How did her desire for independence shape the course of the story, both obviously and more subtly?

3. Do you think Agatha Christie is a good representative of the issues that women faced in her era? Did she have any privileges or responsibilities that set her apart from other women of her period?

4. Describe the night Archie and Agatha first met. How did their relationship change over time, and why? Do you think Agatha's manuscript told the full story? What details do you think she changed or left out? Why do you think she might have altered the "truth"?

5. Archie spends much of the story trying to protect his reputation. Do you think that would be the case if the story took place today? Would it be easier or more difficult for him to deflect guilt in the modern news cycle?

6. What differences did you see between the Agatha within the manuscript and the Agatha who appears at the end of the book? What creative licenses did she take with her own personality and story? Were they justified?

7. Which characters, if any, did you find to be most relatable? Did you connect with Agatha? Were there any characters you wished you knew more about?

8. Agatha left an enormous mark on the mystery community and on the world of books more generally. Do you think her marriage had an effect on her success? Or her disappearance? If so, what was it? How would you characterize her personal and professional legacies?

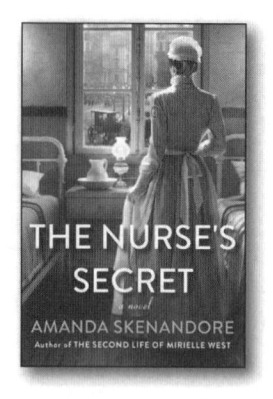

THE NURSE'S SECRET

Amanda Skenandore

From registered nurse Amanda Skenandore, the acclaimed author of *The Second Life of Mirielle West*, a fascinating novel based on the little-known story of America's first nursing school, as a young female grifter in 1880s New York evades the police by conning her way into Bellevue Hospital's training school for nurses...

Based on Florence Nightingale's nursing principles, Bellevue is the first school of its kind in the country. Where once nurses were assumed to be ignorant and unskilled, Bellevue prizes discipline, intellect, and moral character, and only young women of good breeding need apply. At first, Una balks at her prim classmates and the doctors' endless commands. Yet life on the streets has prepared her for the horrors of injury and disease found on the wards, and she slowly gains friendship and self-respect.

Just as she finds her footing, Una's suspicions about a patient's death put her at risk of exposure, and will force her to choose between her instinct for self-preservation, and exposing her identity in order to save others.

Amanda Skenandore brings her medical expertise to a page-turning story that explores the evolution of modern nursing—including the grisly realities of nineteenth-century medicine—as seen through the eyes of an intriguing and dynamic heroine.

"A spellbinding story, a vividly drawn setting, and characters that leap off the pages. This is historical fiction at its finest!" —Sara Ackerman, *USA Today* bestselling author of *The Codebreaker's Secret*

ABOUT THE AUTHOR: **Amanda Skenandore** is an award-winning author of historical fiction and a registered nurse. Her debut novel, *Between Earth and Sky*, was winner of the American Library Association's RUSA Reading List Award and her third novel, *The Second Life of Mirielle West* was the 2023 Silicon Valley Reads Selection, an Apple Best Books of the Month and a Hoopla Book Club Pick. She lives in Las Vegas, Nevada. Visit her online at AmandaSkenandore.com.

June 2022 | Paperback | $16.95 | 9781496726537 | Kensington Books

CONVERSATION STARTERS

1. *The Nurses Secret* offers fascinating glimpse of what life was like for America's very first professional nurses. What were some of the most significant differences you noticed between early nursing as it's represented in the novel and your understanding of the profession today?

2. How has the nursing profession remained the same today as it was 150 years ago?

3. Did the qualifications required to apply to the Bellevue Nurse Training School surprise you?

4. Great wealth and extreme poverty existed side by side in gilded-age New York with almost no middle class in between. The rich lived in European-inspired mansions along Millionaires Row while the poor crowded into tenements—sometimes living a dozen people to a room. How was this reflected in the novel? Does the same degree of class stratification exist today?

5. How did the death of Una's mother shape her outlook?

6. Una has a list of rules to survive life on the streets. How did those rules help her? How did they hurt her? Do you think any of the rules are worth carrying over into her new life?

7. Do you think Edwin and Una are a good fit for each other? Do you think their relationship will endure?

8. Today, nurses are consistently ranked as the number one most trusted profession in America in Gallup's annual poll. Do you feel that distinction is deserved?

9. When Edwin tells Una he doesn't care who knows about their romance, she replies, "Easy for you to say. You don't have anything to lose." What gender dynamics are at play in the novel? Do those same dynamics exist today?

10. Dr. Joseph Lister came to America in 1876 to share his ideas about germ theory and asepsis, but it was several years before the medical community fully embraced his ideas. Why do you think there was such reluctance? Aside from germ theory, what medical advances in the past 150 years do you think have had the biggest impact?

THE PUPPETEER'S DAUGHTERS

Heather Newton

Famed puppeteer and master manipulator Walter Gray surprises his three daughters by announcing there is a fourth at his 80th birthday party. An incomplete paternity test—and a will that places a condition on each daughter's inheritance—suggest that the missing daughter isn't a figment of his dementia.

The three sisters each knew a different version of their enigmatic father, but they all grew up in the presence of fairy tales acted out with marionettes and shadow puppets. If they are to find the fourth daughter and claim the legacy their father has left them, the sisters must confront their fractured relationships with their father and each other.

Infused with fairy tales that occasionally spill magic into the sisters' real lives, *The Puppeteer's Daughters* is a stunningly-woven family saga about the cost and rewards of claiming a creative life.

"*Heartfelt, intriguing and breathtakingly creative.* The Puppeteer's Daughters *proves that happily-ever-afters aren't always the ending to fairytales — sometimes they're just the beginning. Heather Newton is a born storyteller, showing us that magic can spill into our everyday lives when we step out of our comfort zones.*" —**Sarah Addison Allen**, *New York Times* **bestselling** author of *Other Birds*

"*With this mix of traditional fairy tales, offbeat original scripts, insights into the world of puppetry, a touch of* King Lear, *and the basic personality of a romcom,* The Puppeteer's Daughters *is a charming read with some unexpected thoughtfulness between the lines.*" —*New York Journal of Books*

"*A heartwarming story about self-acceptance, forgiveness, and the strings sometimes attached to family love.*" —*Foreword Reviews*

ABOUT THE AUTHOR: **Heather Newton** is the author of *McMullen Circle*, finalist for the W.S. Porter Prize, and *Under the Mercy Trees*, winner of the Thomas Wolfe Memorial Literary Award. Newton is a lawyer, teacher, and co-founder of the Flatiron Writers Room, a nonprofit literary center in Asheville, NC.

July 2022 | Hardcover | $25.99 | 9781684428588 | Keylight Books
May 2023 | Paperback | $15.99 | 9781684428595 | Keylight Books

CONVERSATION STARTERS

1. Now that you've read the novel, go back and reread the epigraph. Why do you think Newton chose this quote?

2. Which sister (Jane, Rosie, or Cora) do you think changes or grows the most by the end of the novel? How do the sisters' relationships with their father, and with each other, change throughout the novel?

3. What do you think of Rosie's "twig house" relationship with Gary?

4. Thievery is a theme in this novel, as is often true in fairy tales. What are some important thefts in the book? How do the thefts affect the thieves and the victims? Why do you think Cora's thefts stop?

5. What do you think Walter's gypsy princess marionette symbolizes for him?

6. What are the respective attitudes of Jane, Cora, Rosie, and Olin toward creativity and claiming a creative life? In what ways (if any) do you think Rosie is creative?

7. In Cora's story, "The Sound Seeker," the Sound Seeker can find lost words. What are some words in your own life that have been lost which you wish you could retrieve?

8. In Cora's variation on the story "Diamonds and Toads," the Reverser of Curses makes the following statement about curses and blessings: "It can be hard to tell the difference at times. These things have two sides, and the side one sees has more to do with the seer than the seen." Do you agree with this statement? Why or why not?

9. Jane's friend Averil says, "At some point, we all have to appreciate what our parents did give us and stop resenting what they couldn't." What do you think Walter was able to give his daughters? What do you think he failed to give them? In your own relationships with your parents or children, what has been given or withheld?

10. Fairy tales often feature encounters with strange folk who are not what they seem. What are some examples of these encounters in the novel? What do you think is the significance of each?

11. What memories do you have of puppets from your childhood?

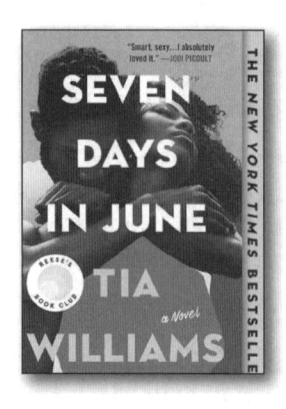

SEVEN DAYS IN JUNE
Tia Williams

The *New York Times* bestseller and Reese Witherspoon book club pick is "a heady combination of book love and between-the-sheets love." (Ruth Ware)

Seven days to fall in love, fifteen years to forget, and seven days to get it all back again...

Eva Mercy is a single mom and bestselling erotica writer who is feeling pressed from all sides. Shane Hall is a reclusive, enigmatic, award-winning novelist.

When Shane and Eva meet unexpectedly at a literary event, sparks fly, raising not only their buried traumas, but the eyebrows of the Black literati. What no one knows is that fifteen years earlier, teenage Eva and Shane spent one crazy, torrid week madly in love. Over the next seven days, Eva and Shane reconnect—but Eva's wary of the man who broke her heart, and she needs a few questions answered...

"A smart, sexy testament to Black joy, to the well of strength from which women draw, and to tragic romances that mature into second chances. I absolutely loved it." —**Jodi Picoult, #1** *New York Times* **bestselling author**

A Best Book of the Year: NPR • *Kirkus* • *Marie Claire* • PopSugar • New York Public Library • Bustle • *Reader's Digest* • Literary Hub

A Best Book of the Summer: *Harper's Bazaar* • *Oprah Daily* • Shondaland • *The Los Angeles Times* • CBS News • *PureWow* • *Good Housekeeping* • BuzzFeed • theSkimm

ABOUT THE AUTHOR: **Tia Williams** had a fifteen year career as a beauty editor for magazines including *Elle*, *Glamour*, *Lucky*, *Teen People*, and *Essence*. In 2004, she pioneered the beauty blog industry with her award winning site, Shake Your Beauty. She wrote the bestselling debut novel *The Accidental Diva* and penned two young adult novels, *It Chicks* and *Sixteen Candles*. Her previous novel, the award winning *The Perfect Find*, is being adapted by Netflix for a film starring Gabrielle Union. Tia is currently an editorial director at Estée Lauder Companies and lives with her daughter and husband in Brooklyn.

June 2022 | Paperback | $16.99 | 9781538719091 | Grand Central Publishing

CONVERSATION STARTERS

1. Eva Mercy is an author who feels creatively stuck, grateful to a series that has made her not only successful and given her a devoted following but also pigeon-holed her as a certain type of writer. Discuss the challenges that artists can experience in changing style.

2. The potential director for the *Cursed* movie adaptation states that the characters need to be white to be "accessible." What are some instances of whitewashing you've witnessed in popular culture? Discuss the repercussions this has on our culture and society.

3. "Your misogynoir is showing" is Eva's response when Khalid denigrates her writing as "fluff." Why do you think a value system has been assigned to different kinds of writing, where genres such as fantasy and romance are seen solely as entertainment and not art? Can you think of ways to combat this perception?

4. Eva and Shane both feel like misfits and outsiders. When they meet, they seem to understand each other on a molecular level. What does *Seven Days in June* make you feel about the importance of being loved and understood by someone else? Discuss what the novel says about allowing yourself to be seen and accepted for who you are.

5. Motherhood, mothering, and what we carry through generations are themes at the core of *Seven Days in June*. Discuss the ways that both Lizette and Eva carry traumas of their ancestors with them, and the ways it makes Eva intent on not repeating the cycle with Audre. How have you seen this play out in your own life, in your relationships with your parents or your children?

6. Shane works with students like Ty to give back to the community and heal from his own childhood trauma. Later, when he decides to coach basketball at the YMCA, he's found a different model of giving back, without creating unhealthy dependencies. Discuss Shane's trajectory over these seven days and the ways in which he grows.

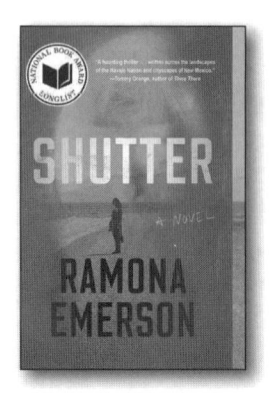

SHUTTER

Ramona Emerson

Longlisted for the National Book Award, this blood-chilling debut set in New Mexico's Navajo Nation is equal parts gripping crime thriller, supernatural horror, and poignant portrayal of coming of age on the reservation.

Rita Todacheene is a forensic photographer working for the Albuquerque police force. Her excellent photography skills have cracked many cases—she is almost supernaturally good at capturing details. In fact, Rita has been hiding a secret: she sees the ghosts of crime victims who point her toward the clues that other investigators overlook. Her taboo and psychologically harrowing ability was what drove her away from the Navajo reservation, where she was raised by her grandmother. It has isolated her from friends and gotten her in trouble with the law. And now it might be what gets her killed.

"This story is way more than a thriller, more than a ghost story. It is one of family and history, of culture, of past and present, of walking set boundaries and of discovering oneself." —*USA Today*

ABOUT THE AUTHOR: **Ramona Emerson** is a *Diné* writer and filmmaker originally from Tohatchi, New Mexico. She has a bachelor's in Media Arts from the University of New Mexico and an MFA in Creative Writing from the Institute of American Indian Arts. She is an Emmy nominee, a Sundance Native Lab Fellow, a Time-Warner Storyteller Fellow, a Tribeca All-Access Grantee and a WGBH Producer Fellow. She currently resides in Albuquerque, New Mexico, where she and her husband, the producer Kelly Byars, run their production company Reel Indian Pictures. *Shutter* is her first novel.

May 2023 | Paperback | $16.95 | 9781641294812 | Soho Crime
August 2022 | Hardcover | $25.95 | 9781641293334 | Soho Crime

CONVERSATION STARTERS

1. What sort of person is Rita? How have the sacrifices she has made for the sake of her family, such as staying in New Mexico for college, shaped her character? If you had her supernatural abilities, how do you think it would affect you—and in contrast, how does it affect Rita? Has her trauma broken her, or strengthened her?

2. *Shutter* is marked by violence and gruesome descriptions of death, but also thoughtful, poignant scenes of a young girl growing up. How would you describe the genre of this book?

3. What do you think Rita should have done about Erma? Rita did feel compelled to help her—but was it out of selflessness, or just because Erma was making her life "a living hell"? How about the rest of the ghosts, who all need help, too? When does asking for help become an act of violence? Is Mr. Bitsilly right when he insists that trying to help these "things" that latch on to Rita is not only pointless, but also dangerous?

4. Do you relate to any of the beliefs expressed in *Shutter* about Death and ghosts. such as the Navajo perspective that these topics are morally wrong and to be avoided at all costs? What are some of the different approaches taken by *Shutter*'s characters to the afterlife?

5. Not everything in Rita's life is gore and ghosts: she also has two close friends, a warm relationship with her supervisor at work, and even a one-night stand with an attractive stranger. Could these people ever truly accept her for who she is, or are there parts of her life that she can never share? What are the risks inherent in Rita being honest about her abilities?

6. How much do you know about life on reservations? Were you surprised by anything you learned from the sections of *Shutter* taking place in Rita's childhood?

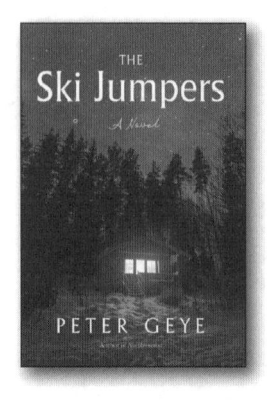

THE SKI JUMPERS

Peter Geye

A brilliant ski jumper has to be fearless—Jon Bargaard remembers this well. His memories of daring leaps and risks might be the key to the book he's always wanted to write: a novel about his family, beginning with Pops, once a champion ski jumper himself, who also took Jon and his younger brother Anton to the heights. But Jon has never been able to get past the next, ruinous episode of their history, and now that he has received a terrible diagnosis, he's afraid he never will.

In a bravura performance, Peter Geye follows Jon deep into the past he tried so hard to leave behind. Traveling back and forth in time, Jon tells his family's story—perhaps his last chance to share it—to his beloved wife Ingrid, circling ever closer to the truth about those events and his own part in them, and revealing the perhaps unforgivable violence done to the brothers' bond.

"Like its ski jumping protagonists, this family saga takes flight with a hammering heart and soars through questions of debt, failure, courage, and reconciliation. It's both distinctly Minnesotan and hugely humane . . . I was deeply moved." — **Kawai Strong Washburn, author of** *Sharks in the Time of Saviors*

"Peter Geye's tender, patient storytelling, exhilarating tension, and indelibly Midwestern characters make The Ski Jumpers *unforgettable."* —**J. Ryan Stradal, author of** *The Lager Queen of Minnesota*

"If you already know his work, this book will surprise and delight you; if you're new to Peter Geye, The Ski Jumpers *is the perfect place to start."* —**Leif Enger, author of** *Virgil Wander*

ABOUT THE AUTHOR: **Peter Geye** is author of the award-winning novels *Safe from the Sea*, *The Lighthouse Road*, *Wintering*, and *Northernmost*. He teaches the yearlong Novel Writing Project at the Loft Literary Center. Born and raised in Minneapolis, he continues to live there with his family.

October 2023 | Paperback | $17.95 | 9781517913502 | University of Minnesota Press

CONVERSATION STARTERS

1. At one point in the novel, the narrator declares, "Every old ski jumper is a liar." Does this cause you to look differently at the stories Jon tells? Does it give you pause when regarding his reliability as a narrator? Does the fact that he's withheld so much from his wife over their long marriage exacerbate your doubt?

2. Complicated family relationships are at the core of this novel. Jon and his brother Anton have been estranged for most of their adult lives. Same with Jon and his mother, Bett. How have these schisms shaped the characters in this novel? Do you have more empathy for certain characters? Why?

3. There are also deep and abiding relationships in this novel, especially between Jon and his own family, including his wife, Ingrid. Despite their closeness, even their dependence on one another, it's also true Jon has kept the biggest secret of his life from her. Does this complicate your feelings about Jon? Does his coming clean with her absolve him of this mistake? At times, Ingrid seems to be roused to anger. What would your response be to the sort of news Jon finally delivers?

4. One of the things Peter Geye is often commended for are his careful descriptions of the north woods, and the shore of Lake Superior in particular. What are some of your favorite descriptions of northern Minnesota in this novel? Or Lake Superior? Is there any significance between those more bucolic settings and the gritty world of the city, especially the Minneapolis bar Anton manages?

5. Ski jumping is more than a subject in the novel. Over the course of the book, it becomes an organizing principle, a cause for reflection—of both regret and great satisfaction—and a source of drama as all three Bargaards compete in fateful competitions. Which of these many experiences resonated the most with you? Which do you think was most meaningful, and why? Which descriptions came closest to giving you the vicarious thrill of participating in the sport yourself?

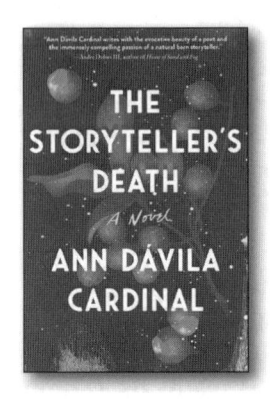

THE STORYTELLER'S DEATH

Ann Dávila Cardinal

BuzzFeed's 20 Highly Anticipated Thrillers of 2022

BookRiot's 15 Best New Mystery Books of 2022

There was always an old woman dying in the back room of her family's house when Isla was a child...

Isla Larsen Sanchez's life begins to unravel when her father passes away. Instead of being comforted at home in New Jersey, her mother starts leaving her in Puerto Rico with her grandmother and great-aunt each summer like a piece of forgotten luggage.

When Isla turns eighteen, her grandmother, a great storyteller, dies. It is then that Isla discovers she has a gift passed down through her family's cuentistas. The tales of dead family storytellers are brought back to life, replaying themselves over and over in front of her.

At first, Isla is enchanted by this connection to the Sanchez cuentistas. But when Isla has a vision of an old murder mystery, she realizes that if she can't solve it to make the loop end, these seemingly harmless stories could cost Isla her life.

"A beautiful book about family, memories, and the power of stories." —*BuzzFeed*

"Mystical, masterful storytelling." —*Ms. Magazine*

"Ann Dávila Cardinal writes with the razored clarity of a surgeon, the spare and evocative beauty of a poet, and the immensely compelling passion of a natural born storyteller. I will gratefully read anything she writes!"—**Andre Dubus III**, *New York Times* bestselling author of *House of Sand and Fog*

ABOUT THE AUTHOR: **Ann Dávila Cardinal** is a novelist and Director of Recruitment for Vermont College of Fine Arts (VCFA) and helped create VCFA's winter MFA in Writing residency in Puerto Rico. She comes from a long line of Puerto Rican writers and one of her two YA horror novels was nominated for a Bram Stroker Award. She lives in Vermont.

October 2022 | Paperback | $16.99 | 9781728250779 | Sourcebooks

CONVERSATION STARTERS

1. Family secrets play a huge role in *The Storyteller's Death*. How do family secrets start and take on a life of their own? Have you ever discovered something shocking about a relative's past that changed your understanding of them? Who are the storytellers in your family?

2. Describe Isla as a character. What circumstances make her an outsider both in Puerto Rico and New Jersey? What is her biggest obstacle?

3. What makes someone a cuentista throughout the story? How do stories gain power even when they aren't strictly true?

4. Alma quickly separates Isla and José when they first meet as children. When you first read that scene, why did you think she stopped their budding friendship? Does knowing more about Alma's own past change your understanding?

5. How do Isla's visions change her view of her family's place in their community? What does she learn about their wealth, politics, and personal pride?

6. The Sanchezes are very proud of their Spanish heritage. Why do Alma and Tío Ramón emphasize this aspect of their lineage? How does that focus on the past contrast with the environment around them?

7. José dismisses Isla at the Partido Popular Democrático rally because he believes her family is pro-statehood. Why does he think that? Why does the PPD oppose the possibility of Puerto Rico becoming a U.S. state?

8. What do quenepas represent for José? How does sharing the fruit with Isla mark a change in their relationship?

9. What motivated Marisol, Alma's sister, to arrange for both Pedro's and her own father's deaths?

10. What's next for the Sanchez family? Do you think they'll be able to follow Isla and Elena's example and move toward greater openness?

SUCH A PRETTY GIRL

Tammy Greenwood

Against the nostalgic grit of 1970s New York City, the precarious lines between girl and woman, art and obscenity, fetish and fame flicker and ignite for a young girl on the brink of stardom and a mother on the verge of collapse in this vividly lyrical drama from award-winning author Tammy Greenwood.

In 1970s New York, her innocence is seductive. Four decades later, it's a crime...

Ryan is eleven in 1976 when she and her mother, an ambitious aspiring actress, move from rural Vermont into to Westbeth Artists Housing in New York City. As her mother dashes from one unsuccessful audition to another, Ryan is left to explore a city coming apart at the seams with crime and corruption, but also bursting with creativity and vibrant color. She longs for safety, comfort, and above all, her mother's attention. But when she's discovered by a talent agent, the spotlight she's thrust into offers a different warmth.

Four decades later, living a quiet life with her daughter in Vermont, the person Ryan is today couldn't be more different from the child star she was in the late 1970s. But when an old photo taken of her as a preteen resurfaces amid accusations that could put her estranged mother in prison, she's forced to revisit her past, reevaluate her relationships, and face the painful truths from that fraught blackout summer of 1977.

"This engrossing novel is a timely look into childhood fame, mother-daughter relationships, and how we consume media." —BuzzFeed, **Best Books of the Month**

ABOUT THE AUTHOR: **Tammy Greenwood** is a four-time San Diego Book Award-winning author and recipient of grants from the Sherwood Anderson Foundation, the Christopher Isherwood Foundation, the National Endowment for the Arts, and the Maryland State Arts Council. She teaches creative writing and lives with her family in San Diego, California. Visit her online at TGreenwood.com

October 2022 | Paperback | $16.95 | 9781496739322 | Kensington Books

CONVERSATION STARTERS

1. *Such a Pretty Girl* explores the relationship between mothers and daughters. In what ways do you think Ryan's parenting of Sasha is a response to her own mother's failures?

2. What was your reaction to Fiona's claim that she was protecting Ryan by making the deal she made with Zev Brenner? Do you think it was true? What were her other motivations?

3. There are two major settings in the novel: Lost River in Vermont and Westbeth in the West Village in NYC. Think about the contrast between these two places, and what each represents to Ryan. Why do you think she fled to Vermont when she leaves her career behind? Which setting did you prefer?

4. The 1970s was a dark time for New York City: it was both morally and financially bankrupt. However, for Ryan and the other children at Westbeth, it is also magical. Discuss the depiction of childhood in this novel. What do you recall about your own childhood?

5. As an adult, Ryan is forced to revisit her childhood through a contemporary lens and is able to see how the adults in her life both failed and exploited her. Is there anything from your own childhood that you now see through a different filter?

6. The modeling industry and the film industry clearly exploit Ryan's innocence and beauty. She argues that Henri really saw her—and that his photos were not exploitative at all. Do you think this is true? Or is it possible that Ryan was wrong about his intentions?

7. Why do you think Ryan kept the secret of what happened on the night of the blackout for so long?

8. Ryan's life is dramatically changed the moment she's "discovered" by Margie. Do you have any moments in your own life that changed your trajectory?

9. This book is also about the various kinds of family's—the ones we are born into and the ones we make. Who do you think is Ryan's "family"? How is her family structure similar to and different from your own?

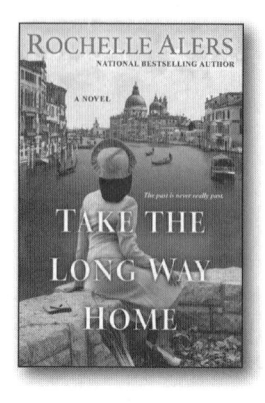

TAKE THE LONG WAY HOME

Rochelle Alers

In an arrestingly vivid novel spanning seven decades and two continents—from a cloistered 1950s Mississippi town founded by formerly enslaved people to the striking diversity of Paris and Rome in the 1960s and 70s, through the flashy glamor of 1980s Wall Street, to present day New York—bestselling author Rochelle Alers chronicles one woman's remarkable journey through some of history's most turbulent eras.

Freedom fighter, brilliant businessperson, devoted wife, master of languages, and ultimately, savior of a European dynasty. Claudia Patterson would become all of these—spurred on by the fiercely powerful loves and losses along the way.

Denny Clark. An abused thirteen-year-old white boy whose life twelve-year-old Claudia saves—complicating her own life for years to come.

Robert Moore. A young Black lawyer who becomes Claudia's beloved husband and partner on the explosive front lines of the Civil Rights Movement. Amid the violence of the Ku Klux Klan, Claudia has a shocking personal encounter—with unimaginable consequences.

Ashley Booth. A Wall Street executive who brings the glamour of New York alive for the now-widowed Claudia, introducing her to an elite circle of Black peers. But their long yet uncommitted romance leads Claudia to move on—to an overseas assignment at an Italian bank.

Giancarlo Pasquale Fortenza. An Italian automobile industrialist, once enamored of a young Claudia—handsome, worldly, and twelve years her senior. A man with whom Claudia reconnects, bringing her life full circle in the boldest, bravest, and most unexpected ways...

ABOUT THE AUTHOR: **Rochelle Alers** is the bestselling author of more than eighty novels with nearly two million copies in print. She is the recipient of numerous awards, including the Golden Pen Award, Emma Award, Vivian Stephens Award, and the Zora Neale Hurston Literary Award. A member of Zeta Phi Beta Sorority, she lives in a charming hamlet on Long Island, NY and can be found online at RochelleAlers.org

October 2023 | Paperback | $16.95 | 9781496735478 | Dafina

CONVERSATION STARTERS

1. When Claudia finds Denny in the woods, do you think Earline is right to take him in? Why or why not?

2. When Claudia gets her period for the first time, her family turns it into a celebration. What did you think about this reaction? What are the rites of passage celebrated in your own family?

3. Did you agree with Claudia's parents' decision to send her to live in Biloxi with Aunt Mavis? Would you have done?

4. At various points in the novel, each if the Bailey women—Claudia, her mother, and her aunts Mavis and Virginia—is referred to as "uppity." Do you agree?

5. Do you think Claudia's aunt should have warned Giancarlo to stop seeing her niece when they first meet in France? How do you think things would have turned out differently if Aunt Virginia hadn't intervened?

6. Claudia learns significant life lessons from the relationships she forms, including those with her close female friends. What do you think is the most important lesson she learned from her college roommate, Yvonne? What about Noel?

7. Though the main characters are fictional, there are many references throughout this novel to real historical figures, such as Thurgood Marshall, Dr. Pauli Murray, Emmett Till, Harlem racketeer Madame Stephanie St. Clair, and many more. Were you unfamiliar with any of the real people who were mentioned in the novel? If so, which ones and what did you learn about them?

8. Throughout the novel, Claudia meets four men who impact her life in crucial ways: Denny, Robert, Ashley, and Giancarlo. What do you think are the best and worst qualities of each man? Why do you think she includes Denny on this list even though he's the only one with whom she didn't fall in love?

9. What do you think is the significance of the novel's title, *Take The Long Way Home*? What is the "home" it refers to?

TALE OF THE DREAMER'S SON

Preeta Samarasan

In what was once a Scottish tea planter's mansion in the highlands of Peninsular Malaysia, all religions are one and race is unheard of. That is, until the occupants of what is now known as the Muhibbah Centre for World Peace are joined by Salmah, a Malay Muslim woman. "All are welcome here," they are reminded by their spiritual leader, Cyril Dragon, who is ignoring news of the changing political climate with its increasing religious intolerance. He is still trying to forget May 13, 1969, when ethnic tensions boiled over into bloodshed.

Tale of the Dreamer's Son guides us from that fateful incident in Malaysian history to the present day. Throughout, Samarasan's polyphonic, rambunctious prose brilliantly navigates the tug-of-war between ideals and reality.

"Samarasan sets a fearless and complex family saga against the social and political upheaval of modern-day Malaysia. The writing is dazzling and poetic; Yusuf's narration soars over place and time and renders the cast with astounding clarity. Fans of Min-Jin Lee, Viet Thanh Nguyen, and Laila Lalami will find much to admire." —**Publishers Weekly, starred review**

"Politics, religion, culture and love collide on every page of Preeta Samarasan's new novel. At once furious and funny, majestic and intimate, Tale of the Dreamer's Son is an ode to the glorious and complex mess that is Malaysia."—**Tash Aw**

ABOUT THE AUTHORS: **Preeta Samarasan** was born in Malaysia. Her first novel, *Evening Is the Whole Day*, was longlisted for the Commonwealth Writers Prize and the Orange Prize for Fiction and won the 2008 Association for Asian American Studies Book Award. Her short fiction has won the Asian American Writers' Workshop Short Story Competition and been selected for a PEN/O. Henry Prize Collection. Her work has been published in *A Public Space*, *Guernica*, *Copper Nickel*, *AGNI*, and other journals. She lives with her family in France.

November 2022 | Paperback | $19.99 | 9781642861204 | World Editions

CONVERSATION STARTERS

1. What did you enjoy most about *Tale of the Dreamer's Son*?

2. Have you had any experience with a tightknit religious community in your life? If so, did you recognize anything?

3. Do you agree with Cyril's "be the change" approach? Should he perhaps have invested all that energy into politics or activism instead?

4. Are all the community members as idealistic? If not, why do you think they're there?

5. Was the death of the Muhibbah Centre for World Peace self-inflicted, or were they hit by forces outside of their control?

6. Why did Leo commit suicide?

7. What was Reza thinking that night? Do you think he knew what Leo might have done?

8. What did Leo and Reza's homosexuality mean to Kannan, if anything?

9. Reza goes through something of a spiritual transformation soon after they all return to the city. Is the change in Kannan as radical?

10. And is Salmah's turn to the national religion a radical break with her past approach to life?

11. What do you make of Kannan's profession? Does it suit him?

12. As a private tutor, does Kannan still let some of his opposition to the rise of the narrow nationalist identity shine through?

13. What does the ending mean to you?

14. The book is ambitious in its attempt to capture a diverse nation, its recent history, and possibly its future. If you are not Malaysian, did it at any point remind you of political or social issues in your own country?

15. Do you feel like you got to know Malaysia, if you didn't know the country somewhat already?

16. Would you be interested in reading more from Preeta Samarasan?

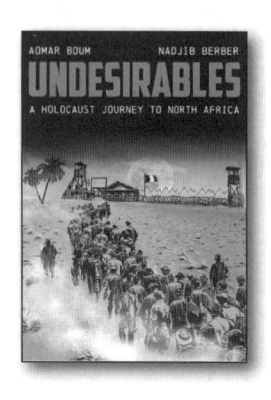

UNDESIRABLES : A HOLOCAUST JOURNEY TO NORTH AFRICA

Aomar Boum, Nadjib Berber (Illustrator)

In this gripping graphic novel, a Jewish journalist encounters an extension of the horrors of the Holocaust in North Africa.

Undesirables follows Hans Frank, a Jewish journalist covering politics in Berlin, who grows increasingly uneasy as he witnesses the Nazi Party consolidate power. Hans flees Germany, ultimately landing in French Algeria just days before the Vichy regime designates all foreign Jews as "undesirables" and calls for their internment. With memories of his former life as a political journalist receding like a dream, Hans spends the next year and a half in forced labor camps, hearing the stories of others whose lives have been upended by violence and war.

Meticulously researched and propulsively written, with bold illustrations that convey the tension of the coming war and the grimness of the Vichy camps, *Undesirables* captures the experiences of thousands of refugees, chronicling how the traumas of the Holocaust extended far beyond the borders of Europe.

"Comprehensive and cinematic, Boum's and Berber's incisive graphic novel illuminates a forgotten and essential story of Holocaust refugees in North Africa." —**David Kushner, author of** *Easy to Learn, Difficult to Master* **and** *Masters of Doom*

"*Undesirables* connects the histories of Jews and North Africans, of antisemitism and racism, of the Holocaust and colonialism in the twentieth century in innovative and surprising ways." —**Michael Brenner, American University, Washington DC and University of Munich**

ABOUT THE AUTHOR: **Aomar Boum** is Maurice Amado Chair in Sephardic Studies in the Departments of Anthropology, Near Eastern Languages and Cultures, and History at the University of California, Los Angeles.

ABOUT THE ILLUSTRATOR: **Nadjib Berber** is an American-Algerian comic artist. He worked as a political cartoonist for the Algerian press (*African Revolution, El Djoumhouria*).

January 2023 | Paperback | $20.00 | 9781503632912 | Stanford University Press

CONVERSATION STARTERS

1. Why do you think Boum and Berber chose a graphic format to tell this story? Do you agree with their choice? Why or why not?

2. There are several panels throughout the book which include untranslated German. Why do you think Boum chose to leave them untranslated? Did these panels strike you differently from the ones translated into or written solely in English? How so?

3. Towards the beginning of the book, we spend time with our narrator, Hans, and his father, who discuss the beginnings of Hitler's takeover of Germany. What factors do you believe are most critical to the strikingly disparate opinions Hans and his father have regarding what is happening? Why, despite these differences, do you think both are still in Germany?

4. During his visit to Paris in 1933, Sultan Sidi Mohammed Ben Youssef notes that he is "troubled by the strategy of division that European settlers in some cities in Morocco are pushing these days…I am worried about how this is affecting the relationship between my Muslim and Jewish subjects." Do you believe this strategy is limited to Youssef's time or location? If so, why? If not, where and how do you see this strategy in use?

5. Despite the fact that they were all interned at the same camp, the work and treatment of different groups of internees at Djelfa was very different—the French, for example, experienced much better conditions than their Spanish counterparts. What purpose did this division serve?

6. How do the conditions in Djelfa's labor camp compare to what you know of the conditions in German labor camps? Does this tell you anything about the governments which oversaw them?

7. Hans' escape from Djenien-bou-rezg shows that, regardless of how awful or dangerous things became during the war, good people remained willing to do the right thing. Still, with the threat of internment or death hovering over every resistance member, what do you think inspired them to continue to fight? To save others?

8. Why do you think Boum and Berber chose to end the book with the arrival of Americans to Africa instead of following Hans through the end of the war? What would even qualify as 'the end' for people like Hans?

ReadingGroupChoices.com

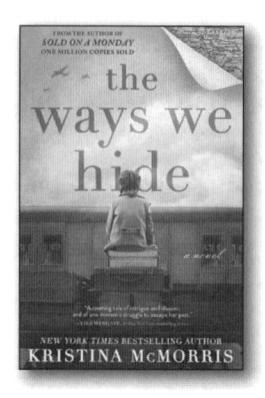

THE WAYS WE HIDE

Kristina McMorris

From the *New York Times* bestselling author of *Sold On A Monday*

As a little girl raised amid the hardships of Michigan's Copper Country, Fenna Vos learned to focus on her own survival. That ability sustains her even now as the Second World War rages in faraway countries. Though she performs onstage as the assistant to an unruly escape artist, behind the curtain she's the mastermind of their act.

Fenna doesn't foresee being called upon by British military intelligence and being tasked with designing escape aids to thwart the Germans, but reluctantly joins the unconventional team as an inventor. But when a test of her loyalty draws her deep into the fray, she discovers no mission is more treacherous than escaping one's past.

Inspired by stunning true accounts, *The Ways We Hide* is a gripping story of love and loss, the wars we fight—on the battlefields and within ourselves—and the courage found in unexpected places.

"*The Queen's Gambit* meets *The Alice Network* in this epic, action-packed novel of family, loss, and one woman's journey to save all she holds dear including freedom itself." —**Kristin Harmel**, *New York Times* bestselling author of *The Forest of Vanishing Stars*

"A riveting tale of intrigue and illusion, danger and historical mystery, but at its heart the story of one woman's struggle to escape her own past." —**Lisa Wingate** #1 *New York Times* bestselling author of *Before We Were Yours*

"Just like her heroine, Kristina McMorris works magic in this twisting tale of James Bond's Q meets World War II. I love this book! —**Kate Quinn**, *New York Times* bestselling author of *The Rose Code* and *The Diamond Eye*

ABOUT THE AUTHOR: **Kristina McMorris** is a *New York Times* and *USA Today* bestselling author and her novels have garnered more than twenty national literary awards. She lives with her husband and two sons in Oregon.

September 2022 | Hardcover | $27.99 | 9781728249797 | Sourcebooks
September 2022 | Paperback | $16.99 | 9781728249766 | Sourcebooks

CONVERSATION STARTERS

1. Did your impression of the child on the cover change by the novel's end? What about the title? Describe the various meanings it holds throughout the story.

2. From the Italian Hall Disaster and its parallel tragedy at Bethnal Green Station to the efforts of MI9, Houdini, and the Dutch Resistance, plus those of the Engelandvaarders, *The Ways We Hide* highlights myriad stunning pieces of history. Which among them fascinated and/or surprised you most?

3. Love, loss, family, and sacrifice are major themes of the novel and the driving force behind many of Fenna's and Arie's actions. Did you largely agree or disagree with Fenna's decisions? What about Arie's?

4. Several objects throughout the story—including the toy train, buttons, and, most frequently, a ball of string—help forge lasting bonds between characters. Which item was your favorite? Likewise, which possessions in your own life carry deep senti¬mental value given their link to a person or relationship?

5. Were you familiar with MI9 prior to reading this book? Which gadgets did you enjoy learning about most?

6. From Fenna's childhood, the stampede on Christmas Eve contributed significantly to shaping her life, even decades later. What childhood experience(s) most altered your own life? Were there resulting obstacles you later learned to overcome?

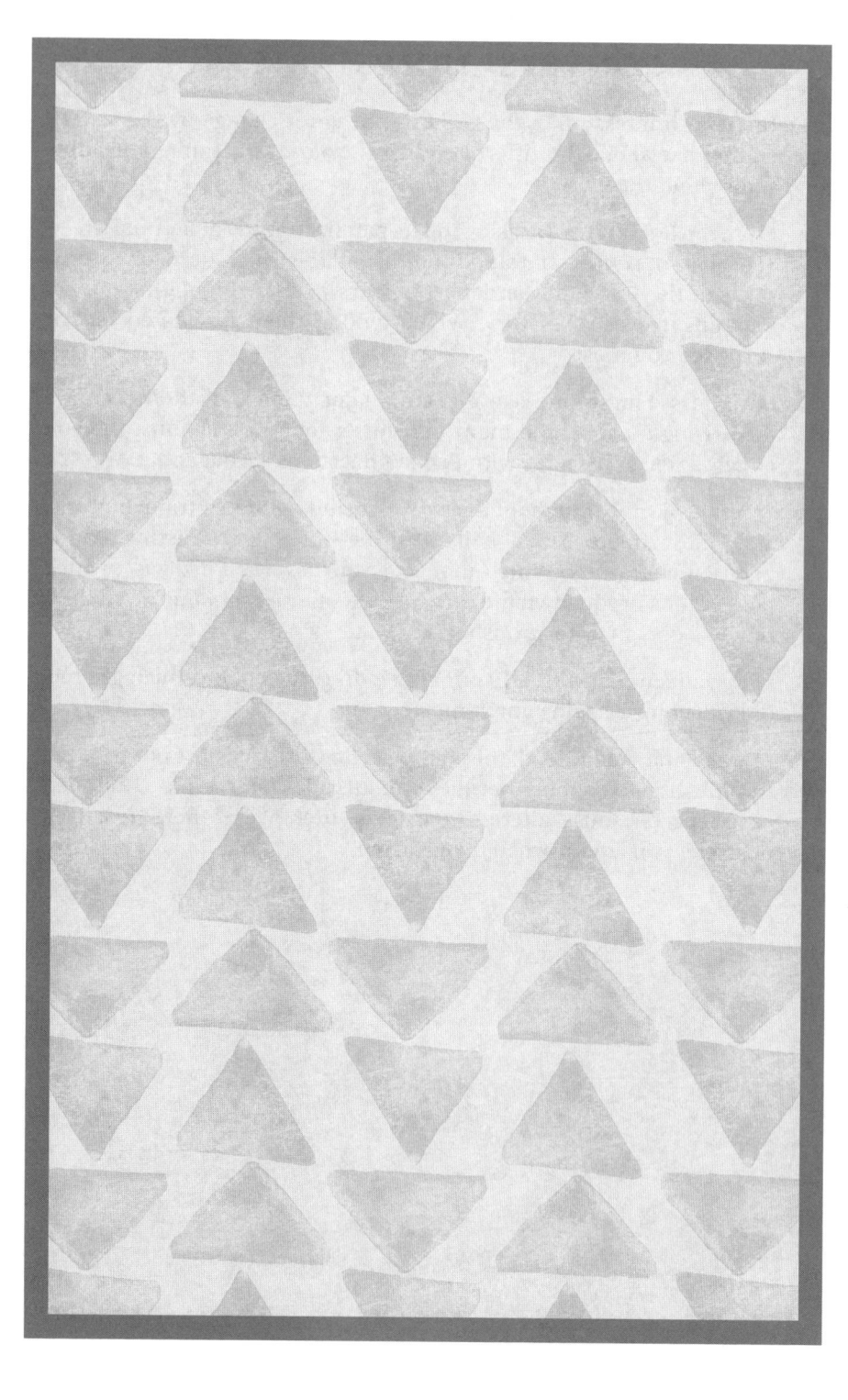

NONFICTION

ANIMAL JOY: A BOOK OF LAUGHTER AND RESUSCITATION
Nuar Alsadir

Laughter shakes us out of our deadness. An outburst of spontaneous laughter is an eruption from the unconscious that, like political resistance, poetry, or self-revelation, expresses a provocative, impish drive to burst free from external constraints. Taking laughter's revelatory capacity as a starting point, and rooted in Nuar Alsadir's experience as a poet and psychoanalyst, *Animal Joy* seeks to recover the sensation of being present and embodied.

Writing in a poetic, associative style, blending the personal with the theoretical, Alsadir ranges from her experience in clown school, Freud's un-Freudian behaviors, marriage brokers and war brokers, to "Not Jokes," Abu Ghraib, the Brett Kavanaugh hearings, laugh tracks, and how poetry can wake us up. At the center of the book, however, is the author's relationship with her daughters, who erupt into the text like sudden, unexpected laughter. These interventions—frank, tender, and always a challenge to the writer and her thinking—are like tiny revolutions, pointedly showing the dangers of being severed from one's true self and hinting at ways one might be called back to it.

"*Animal Joy jumps for intellectual joy, hopscotching from literary criticism to philosophy and psychology to political analysis. . . . Yet, by sleight of pen, these philosophy-laden pages remain light and graceful. . . . The book is in effect a gift to the courageous. It offers an opportunity for self-reflection and growth. . . . Great art mainly makes you not think but feel.* Animal Joy *made me do both.*" —**Melissa Holbrook Pierson**, *The Washington Post*

ABOUT THE AUTHOR: **Nuar Alsadir**, a poet and psychoanalyst, is the author of *Fourth Person Singular*, a finalist for the National Book Critics Circle Award in Poetry and the Forward Prize for Best Collection, and *More Shadow Than Bird*. She lives in New York City.

August 2022 | Paperback | $16.00 | 9781644450932 | Graywolf Press

CONVERSATION STARTERS

1. What did Nuar Alsadir learn in clown school that she extrapolates into life lessons?

2. What are some of the connections Alsadir draws between clowning, poetry, and psychoanalysis?

3. Did *Animal Joy* change your perception of laughter? If so, how?

4. Name three or more examples from *Animal Joy* of how laughter can be a form of resistance

5. How does Alsadir define the True and False Selves, borrowing from the psychoanalyst Winnicott? What are some of the benefits of being connected to your True Self, and what are some of the dangers in being severed from it?

6. *Animal Joy's* subtitle is "A Book of Laughter and Resuscitation." What does laughter have to do with resuscitation?

7. Alsadir discusses the use of a laugh track and explains how different laugh sounds can be used to manipulate the reaction of an audience. What are some of the examples Alsadir shares of how the laughter of others affects us and how that can be used strategically, not only on television but in the interpersonal and political realms?

8. *Animal Joy* explores why it is so important to understand what kind of laughter you are hearing. Name 3-5 various types of laughter, as well as their intentions and effects.

9. On page 102, Alsadir defines Duchenne laughter as "spontaneous, body-driven laughter. . . . that often breaks through censors and other inhibitory processes." Can you give examples from your own experience of this kind of laughter? How frequently do you experience Duchenne laughter and can you notice any commonalities between the contexts in which it erupts?

10. Alsadir's focus is not only on spontaneous fits of laughter but spontaneous gestures and expressions more broadly. What does Alsadir think we can learn from spontaneous actions—even bungled ones, like slips of the tongue?

11. Other examples in the book come from Alsadir's experiences with her two daughters. What do children in particular have to teach us about laughter and how it functions?

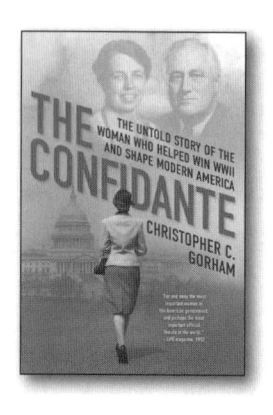

THE CONFIDANTE: THE UNTOLD STORY OF THE WOMAN WHO HELPED WIN WWII AND SHAPE MODERN AMERICA

Christopher C. Gorham

The first-ever biography of Anna Marie Rosenberg, a Hungarian Jewish immigrant with only a high school education who went on to be dubbed by *Life* magazine "the most important woman in the American government, and perhaps the most important official female in the world." Her life ran parallel to the front lines of history yet—her influence on 20th century America, from the New Deal to the Cold War and beyond, has never before been told.

For readers of *Hidden Figures*, *A Woman of No Importance*, and *Eleanor: A Life*, the previously unrecognized life of Anna Rosenberg is extraordinary, inspiring, and uniquely American.

As FDR's special envoy to Europe in World War II, she went where FDR couldn't go. She was among the first Allied women to enter a liberated concentration camp. She stood in the Eagle's Nest, Hitler's mountain retreat, days after its capture. She guided the direction of the G.I. Bill of Rights and the Manhattan Project. A force for labor unions, national healthcare, women's equality, and racial integration, she ultimately was appointed to U.S. assistant secretary of defense.

Though Anna Rosenberg emerged from modest immigrant beginnings, equipped with only a high school education, she was the real power behind national policies critical to America winning WWII and prospering afterwards. Astonishingly, her story remains largely ignored – until now. In this inspiring, impeccably researched, and revelatory book, Christopher C. Gorham at last brings Anna Rosenberg the recognition she so richly deserves.

"Mr. Gorham's biography is also a mystery. How could we have forgotten such a woman?...What *The Confidante* provides, with cinematic color and encyclopedic clarity, is a resurrection of that history." — *The Wall Street Journal*

ABOUT THE AUTHOR: **Christopher C. Gorham** is a lawyer and teacher of modern American history at Westford Academy. He lives with his wife in Massachusetts and can be found online at ChristopherCGorham.com.

March 2023 | Hardcover | $28.99 | 9780806542003 | Kensington
May 2024 | Paperback | $16.95 | 9780806542027 | Kensington

CONVERSATION STARTERS

1. Anna Rosenberg became FDR's closest advisor during World War II, the second-highest ranking woman ever to serve in the US government and, according to Life, " perhaps the most important official female in the world." Despite her tremendous accomplishments, Anna Rosenberg remains largely unknown to most people. Why do you think there isn't more awareness of Anna Rosenberg's contributions to 20th century America?

2. How do you think Anna Rosenberg's experiences and trials as a young woman in New York City prepared her for enduring success in business and politics?

3. In what ways do you think Anna Rosenberg's immigrant background informed her patriotism?

4. Anna split time between New York and Washington, and often came across as "unattached." Do you believe this was a help or a hindrance in her career?

5. Rosenberg was told at an early age that women in politics achieve more "behind the scenes." How does this make you think about the use and impact of hard-power and soft-power?

6. Anna recognized the link between social equality and a stronger democracy. How did her actions support civil rights for Black Americans and for American women?

7. When Anna's fierce loyalty to her new country was challenged by Senator Joe McCarthy, why do you believe she withstood the attack when other women's careers were prematurely ended?

8. What was it about Anna Rosenberg's personality that made her a trusted friend to not only FDR, but presidents Truman, Eisenhower, and Johnson?

9. After WWII, Anna was distraught to find the WACs and WAVES treated differently than their male veteran counterparts. What was behind this mistreatment?

10. Anna was urged to write her memoirs by Eleanor Roosevelt and leading publishing houses, with Edward R. Murrow once telling her, "You have quite a book to write someday." Why do you think Anna resisted this so strongly?

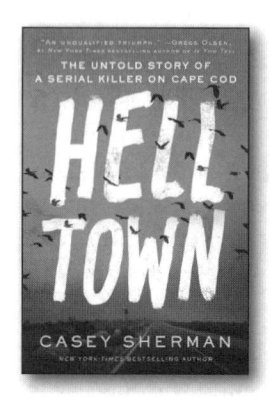

HELLTOWN

Casey Sherman

1969: The hippie scene is vibrant in Provincetown, Massachusetts. Long-haired teenagers roam the streets, strumming guitars and preaching about peace and love... and Tony Costa is at the center of it all.

To a certain group of smitten young women, he is known as Sire—the leader of their counterculture movement, the charming man who speaks eloquently and hands out hallucinogenic drugs like candy. But beneath his benign persona lies a twisted and uncontrollable rage that threatens to break loose at any moment. Tony Costa is the most dangerous man on Cape Cod, and no one who crosses his path is safe.

When young women begin to disappear, Costa's natural charisma and good looks initially protect him from suspicion. But as the bodies are discovered, the police close in on him as the key suspect. Meanwhile, local writers Kurt Vonnegut and Norman Mailer are locked in a desperate race to secure their legacies as great literary icons—and they both set their sights on Tony Costa and the drug-soaked hippie culture that he embodies as their next promising subject, launching independent investigations that stoke the competitive fires between two of the greatest American writers.

Immersive, unflinching, and shocking, *Helltown* reveals the secrets of a notorious serial killer and unspools the threads connecting Costa, Vonnegut, and Mailer in the seaside city that played host to horrors unlike any ever seen before.

"Utterly absorbing... Destined to be on all the year-end best nonfiction lists!" —**Gregg Olsen, #1** *New York Times* **bestselling author of** *If You Tell*

"Casey Sherman is a master at bringing history alive. Compelling, complex, and revealing—do not miss this!" —**Hank Phillippi Ryan,** *USA Today* **bestselling author of** *Her Perfect Life*

ABOUT THE AUTHOR: **Casey Sherman** is an American author, journalist, and screenwriter.

July 2022 | Hardcover | $26.99 | 9781728245959 | Sourcebooks
May 2023 | Paperback | $18.99 | 9781728271934 | Sourcebooks

CONVERSATION STARTERS

1. How did the hippie culture of the late '60s disguise disappearances? Why didn't police prioritize disappearances like Sydney Monzon's?

2. What drew Tony Costa's "disciples" to him? Did anyone take their defense of him seriously?

3. Costa was not particularly neat about his crimes, so why did it take so long for him to be apprehended? Why did he volunteer to speak to police after successfully disappearing?

4. Mailer questioned whether he would be capable of a crime like Costa's. What comparisons can you make between Vonnegut's, Mailer's, and Costa's erratic behavior? Do you think there is a significant difference between the three men?

5. The police were determined to pin Costa with Mary Anna and Pat's murders, even when they'd only found a third, unrelated corpse. How did that change the way they investigated? What do you think of that approach more generally?

6. Why does Costa view Cory Devereaux as his rival? What does Devereaux think of Costa?

7. What was District Attorney Ed Dinis's motivation for taking on Tony Costa's prosecution? Why did he exaggerate the already extensive mutilation of the girls' bodies? Did he ultimately succeed in his goal?

8. Why were writers like Evelyn Lawson convinced that witchcraft was involved in the Truro murders? What appeal did that explanation have for people like Norman Mailer?

9. Dinis chose not to prosecute all four murders, sticking with Pat Walsh and Mary Ann Wysocki's deaths which he called "slam dunks". Why did he make that decision? Do you think justice is better served by a trial for all crimes that ends without a conviction or a trial for some crimes that results in a sentence?

10. During the trial, Costa's lawyers assert that his drug use is to blame for his transgressions. How does that reflect the general attitude towards drugs at the time? Do you think his defense would use that tactic if he were on trial today?

LAST TO EAT, LAST TO LEARN: MY LIFE IN AFGHANISTAN FIGHTING TO EDUCATE WOMEN

Pashtana Durrani, Tamara Bralo

From young Afghan activist Pashtana Durrani, a deeply inspiring memoir about the power of learning and the value of educators in their many forms—from teachers, mentors, and role models, to fathers, mothers, and any one of us with the drive to stand against ignorance.

Since childhood, Pashtana Durrani has recognized her calling: to educate Afghanistan's girls and young women. In a country devastated by war and violence, where girls are often married off before reaching their teenage years, heeding that call seemed close to impossible. But Pashtana's story is as singular as her ambition.

Raised in an Afghan refugee camp in Pakistan where her father, a tribal leader, founded a community school for girls within their home, Pashtana was just seven when she began teaching, sharing everything she learned in her private English lessons. At sixteen, she was admitted to a preparatory program to study at Oxford, but turned it down to travel to Afghanistan and begin her mission.

There, Pashtana founded the nonprofit LEARN and developed a brilliant program for getting educational materials directly into the hands of girls in remote areas. Though Pashtana herself was ruthlessly targeted when the Taliban returned to power, she continues to fight for women's education and autonomy in Afghanistan and beyond.

"I hope readers will be inspired by Pashtana's mission to give every girl the education she deserves and the opportunity to pursue her dreams. —**Malala Yousafzai**

ABOUT THE AUTHORS: **Pashtana Durrani** is an Afghan education activist, founder of the NGO LEARN, and a Malala's Fund Education Champion.

Tamara Bralo is an award-winning journalist and spent years covering war zones around the world. She currently works as a media consultant for safety and investigative reporting; and for Undivided, an NGO promoting women's perspectives and narratives of war.

February 2024 | Hardcover | $28.00 | 9780806542447 | Citadel Press

CONVERSATION STARTERS

1. Many women mentioned in *Last to Eat, Last to Learn* experience domestic violence at least once in their lives. What do you think are the root causes of such wide-spread domestic violence against women in Afghanistan? What, if anything, could be done to improve the situation? Do you think Pashtana's idea of fostering a sense of solidarity among those who fall victims to domestic abuse is a viable one?

2. Pashtana says her activism was a product of her circumstances rather than a choice. At the same time, strong-willed and utterly unwilling to accept her role as a woman as dictated by the Afghan norms, she is anything but defined by her circumstances. What else do you think contributed to Pashtana's path to activism? How does this make you think about your freedoms and how you have been defined by your own circumstances?

3. Tribalism usually has negative connotations in Western societies, but Pashtana's story is a love letter not only to her own tribe, but to the system itself. She defends the structure of tribalism and finds it not only redeemable, but valuable. Do you agree with her assessment? Do you think tribal structures could be compatible with the modern world?

4. Pashtana's incredible relationship with her father is a cornerstone of her memoir. From the moment Pashtana was born, he contravenes the traditional Afghan views on daughters: he celebrates her and he insists she shouldn't be called 'the girl' but rather his 'child'. How much influence do you think her father's insistence on Pashtana's equality influenced her own thinking and how she came to see herself? How much did it equip her to attempt her fight the system? Who in your own life has been instrumental in transforming your identity, and why?

5. Pashtana talks about access to education being weaponized, especially in rural areas. Is education the catalyst of societal change? Do you agree with Pashtana's notion that denying access to education is ultimately a political act? If so, what needs to change to make it more accessible?

THE RED WIDOW: THE SCANDAL THAT SHOOK PARIS AND THE WOMAN BEHIND IT ALL

Sarah Horowitz

Paris, 1889: Margeurite Steinheil is a woman with ambition. But having been born into a middle-class family and trapped in a marriage to a failed artist twenty years her senior, she knows her options are limited.

Determined to fashion herself into a new woman, Meg orchestrates a scandalous plan with her most powerful resource: her body. Amid the dazzling glamor, art, and romance of bourgeois Paris, she takes elite men as her lovers. Her ambitions, though, go far beyond becoming the most desirable woman in Paris; at her core, she is a woman determined to conquer French high society. But the game she plays is a perilous one: navigating misogynistic double-standards, public scrutiny, and political intrigue, she is soon vaulted into infamy in the most dangerous way possible.

A real-life femme fatale, Meg influences government positions and resorts to blackmail—and maybe even poisoning—to get her way. Leaving a trail of death and disaster in her wake, she earns the name the "Red Widow". With the police baffled and the public enraged, Meg breaks every rule in the bourgeois handbook and becomes the most notorious woman in Paris.

"*A fascinating woman, a figure at once seductive, hysterical, adulterous, mendacious, captivating and cultured.*" —**The** *New York Times*

"Plenty of salacious tidbits make The Red Widow fun to read, but Ms. Horowitz... delivers more than a lurid tale of murder. She examines the moral attitude of a society in which women like Steinheil had little independence and were forced to rely on men for their survival." —**The Wall Street Journal**

ABOUT THE AUTHOR: **Sarah Horowitz** has a PhD in modern European history from UC Berkeley and is core faculty in Women's, Gender, and Sexuality Studies at Washington and Lee University.

September 2022 | Hardcover | $26.99 | 9781728226323 | Sourcebooks
October 2023 | Paperback | $17.99 | 9781728280332 | Sourcebooks

CONVERSATION STARTERS

1. The marriage between Meg and Adolphe was contentious for a few reasons. What were they?

2. Discuss Meg's upbringing and family dynamic. How do you think it influenced her behavior as an adult?

3. How were different social classes popularly characterized in nineteenth-century France? Were these depictions accurate?

4. Meg wielded her sexuality to climb the social ladder. In what ways was she successful? In what ways did her sexual barter system backfire?

5. Characterize Meg's feelings for Adolphe, Felix, and Emile. How did her feelings differ from man to man?

6. What are the prevailing theories regarding Adolphe's and Emilie's murders? Which do you think is the truth?

7. As a woman (with a working-class mother), Meg understood what it meant to be marginalized, yet she still disdained other oppressed groups, including Jews and the lower classes. Why do you think that is?

8. Discuss the role media played in the Steinheil Affair. Did they make the situation better or worse? Can you draw any parallels to today's media?

9. In what ways do you think the trial and Meg's time in prison changed her?

10. Meg became a celebrity but never wanted to be one. Can you think of other women today who became famous without wanting to be? How might their stories be similar to Meg's?

11. Meg was simultaneously loved and hated by the public. Why do you think that is? After learning her entire story, how do you feel about her?

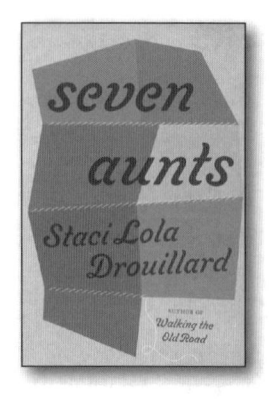

SEVEN AUNTS

Staci Lola Drouillard

Minnesota Book Award for Memoir & Creative Nonfiction

They were German and English, Anishinaabe and French, born in the north woods and Midwestern farm country. They moved again and again, and they fought for each other when men turned mean, when money ran out, when babies—and there were so many—added more trouble but even more love. These are the aunties: Faye, who lived in California, and Lila, who lived just down the street; Doreen, who took on the bullies taunting her "mixed-blood" brothers and sisters; Gloria, who raised six children; Betty, who left a marriage of indenture to a misogynistic southerner to find love and acceptance with a Norwegian logger; and Carol and Diane, who broke the warped molds of their own upbringing.

From the fabric of these women's lives, Staci Lola Drouillard stitches a colorful quilt, its brightly patterned pieces as different as her aunties, yet alike in their warmth and spirit and resilience, their persistence in speaking for their generation. *Seven Aunts* is an inspired patchwork of memoir and reminiscence, poetry, testimony, love letters, and family lore.

"Far more than a family history, Seven Aunts *is an honor song that reveals the everyday heroism of these women's lives.*" —**Diane Wilson, author of** *The Seed Keeper*

"Mesmerizing. A family story at once vast and intimate, it's also a book about womanhood and mothering, the confluence of Native American and settler lives, and the resplendent, beautiful northern third of Minnesota." —**Peter Geye, author of** *Northernmost*

"In this unique and compelling memoir, Staci Lola Drouillard tells the story of her seven aunts—Anishinaabe and European—whose strength, spirit, and determination to thrive illustrate that of so many other women throughout history." —**Ms. Magazine**

ABOUT THE AUTHOR: **Staci Lola Drouillard,** a descendant of the Grand Portage Band of Lake Superior Anishinaabe, is the award-winning author of *Walking the Old Road: A People's History of Chippewa City and the Grand Marais Anishinaabe.*

June 2022 | Paperback | $21.95 | 9781517912857 | University of Minnesota Press

CONVERSATION STARTERS

1. Faye was said to be afflicted with a condition the author calls the "morbidity of motherhood." Discuss the ways that girls like Faye are groomed for motherhood from a young age and how that expectation shaped Faye's life in both positive and negative ways. Follow up question: Do you think Faye was a good mother?

2. The battle for women's rights and bodily autonomy continues to be fought, not just here in the U.S. but also around the world. As character studies for the future of women's rights, how do the seven women profiled in the book fit into the larger discussion about women's right to choose whether or not to have children (e.g. Carol's experiences as an unwed mother in the 1950s)?

3. Let's talk about women and food, which is another important theme throughout the book. What are some of the stories related to food (and the eating, or not eating, of it) that resonated with you? Follow up question: Is there an antidote to the phenomenon of "fatthrowing"?

4. Feeding people and "bringing warmth" is traditionally the work of women, especially for rural families with a lot of children. For both families profiled in *Seven Aunts*, food is also equated with love and affection. How was this dynamic problematic for Doreen, in particular?

5. Diane, in particular, tried to break free of patriarchal expectations about women and what society views as "normative" culture. Do you feel that she was successful in doing that? Follow up question: Were there repercussions for any of the aunties when they tried to break free of societal expectations?

6. This is fundamentally a book about women, but to really understand the life stories presented in the book, we also must learn about the men in their lives. The fathers, brothers, and husbands. Take some time to discuss the role of men in each chapter of the book. Examples: What man played the biggest role in Faye's life? What man changed Lila's life the most? Who might Gloria have done best without?

7. Talk about the role of truth-telling as it relates to family stories and women's lives. Is there any danger in telling the truth? Why or why not?

UNCOMMON MEASURE: A JOURNEY THROUGH MUSIC, PERFORMANCE, AND THE SCIENCE OF TIME

Natalie Hodges

National Book Award Longlist

New York Times "Editors' Choice" selection

A virtuosic debut from a gifted violinist searching for a new mode of artistic becoming.

How does time shape consciousness and consciousness, time? Do we live in time, or does time live in us? And how does music, with its patterns of rhythm and harmony, inform our experience of time?

Uncommon Measure explores these questions from the perspective of a young Korean American who dedicated herself to perfecting her art until performance anxiety forced her to give up the dream of becoming a concert solo violinist. Anchoring her story in illuminating research in neuroscience and quantum physics, Hodges traces her own passage through difficult family dynamics, prejudice, and enormous personal expectations to come to terms with the meaning of a life reimagined—one still shaped by classical music but moving toward the freedom of improvisation.

"Uncommon and genre-defying." —Alexandra Jacobs, *New York Times*

"Incandescent." —Kat Chow, *New York Times Book Review*

"Hodges considers the elemental truth pulsating beneath our experience of music and of our very lives." —Maria Popova, *Marginalian*

ABOUT THE AUTHOR: **Natalie Hodges** has performed as a classical violinist throughout Colorado and in New York, Boston, Paris, and the Italian Piedmont, as well as at the Aspen Music Festival and the Stowe Tango Music Festival. She is a graduate of Harvard University, where she studied English and music, and currently lives in Boulder, Colorado. *Uncommon Measure* is her first book.

March 2022 | Paperback | $17.99 | 9781942658979 | Bellevue Literary Press

CONVERSATION STARTERS

1. The *New York Times* lauds *Uncommon Measure* as "a genre-defying memoir." How does the author's personal narrative intertwine with the psychological and scientific concepts she illuminates? How would you classify Hodges's merging of memory, music, and scientific investigation?

2. Hodges describes classical music as a genre "at the dusty peak of Western high art, one in which contemporary American culture is increasingly less interested." Have Hodges's reflections enhanced your appreciation for it?

3. On top of the immense stress of striving to become a soloist, Hodges feels the added pressure of being a "model minority." How does her experience as a Korean American shape her relationship with classical music? How do the internal pressures of her family and the external force of assimilation influence her identity?

4. The author has a complex relationship with her beloved mother: "She gives, I take: that has always been the imbalanced equation of our relationship, its asymmetry and equilibrium." Is this imbalance inherent in the mother/daughter relationship? Do you agree that there must always be a "frightening asymmetry at the heart of love"?

5. As Hodges mourns the loss of her identity as a violinist, she writes, "I felt haunted by a monumental sense of failure, of aborted struggle and lost time." Yet she found new joy and freedom in jazz, tango, and the magic of time's smooth movement during improvisation. What is your experience of time and improvisational flow? Have you ever felt time moving differently? Is time ever truly lost?

6. What new ideas did *Uncommon Measure* spark within you about creativity, the ways science and art are connected, and the way our brains experience conditions such as performance anxiety?

7. Hodges opens and closes the book with the same idea. Connecting our subjective experience of time with a revolutionary physics experiment, she concludes, "If you want to change the past, all you have to do is try to record what happened in it." Do you agree? In writing this book, has she changed her own past?

VOICE OF THE FISH: A LYRIC ESSAY

Lars Horn

Lars Horn's *Voice of the Fish*, the latest Graywolf Press Nonfiction Prize winner, is an interwoven essay collection that explores the trans experience through themes of water, fish, and mythology, set against the backdrop of travels in Russia and a debilitating back injury that left Horn temporarily unable to speak. In Horn's adept hands, the collection takes shape as a unified book: short vignettes about fish, reliquaries, and antiquities serve as interludes between longer essays, knitting together a sinuous, wave-like form that flows across the book.

Horn swims through a range of subjects, roving across marine history, theology, questions of the body and gender, sexuality, transmasculinity, and illness. From Horn's upbringing with a mother who used them as a model in photos and art installations—memorably in a photography session in an ice bath with dead squid—to Horn's travels before they were out as trans, these essays are linked by a desire to interrogate liminal physicalities. Horn reexamines the oft-presumed uniformity of bodily experience, breaking down the implied singularity of "the body" as cultural and scientific object. The essays instead privilege ways of seeing and being that resist binaries, ways that falter, fracture, mutate. A sui generis work of nonfiction, *Voice of the Fish* blends the aquatic, mystical, and physical to reach a place beyond them all.

"Horn offers fascinating piscine lore, rendered in prose that's grounded and evocative even when hallucinatory. The result is a sonorous meditation on living a fluid life." —**Publishers Weekly**

ABOUT THE AUTHOR: **Lars Horn** holds MAs from the University of Edinburgh; the École normale supérieure, Paris; and Concordia University, Montreal. Horn's work has appeared in the *Kenyon Review*, *Write Across Canada*, and *New Writing Scotland*. They live in Miami.

June 2022 | Paperback | $16.00 | 9781644450895 | Graywolf Press

CONVERSATION STARTERS

1. *Voice of the Fish* touches on numerous subjects, from classical literature to mythology to actual fish. What links do you see between these themes?

2. *Voice of the Fish* intersperses longer narrative sections with shorter explorations of various topics and events. How does this structure strengthen Horn's project as a whole? How does this approach differ from a more linear narrative?

3. Some of the most striking images in the book involve Horn modeling for their mother's photography and having their body cast for sculptural works. How do those experiences relate to Horn's sense of their own body? How do these artworks connect to Horn's sense of the divide between interiors and exteriors?

4. This is a work of nonfiction that is both deeply personal and heavily researched. How do these two aspects complement each other?

5. Rather than "artwork as the static end of a creative process," Lars Horn expresses their attraction and commitment to "artwork as a creative process" (38). How does *Voice of the Fish* embody this distinction?

6. How does Horn's trip to Georgia connect them back to both an earlier time and an earlier version of themselves? What part does the speaking of Russian play?

7. Aquatic life and aquariums figure throughout the book. How might the threaded essay itself function as an aquarium?

8. Horn's loss of language was a major life event. How do you think losing and then regaining their voice shaped this book?

9. What are some of the ways Horn defines fluidity? How do they describe and explore its characteristics and effects? How do these approaches compare and contrast to your own definitions of fluidity?

10. On page 7 Horn states, "Nonbinary, transmasculine—my gender exists, for the most part, as unseen, unworded, unintelligible. . . ." What might gender look like written beyond the blurring of a male-female binary?" How does *Voice of the Fish* deliver answers to this question?

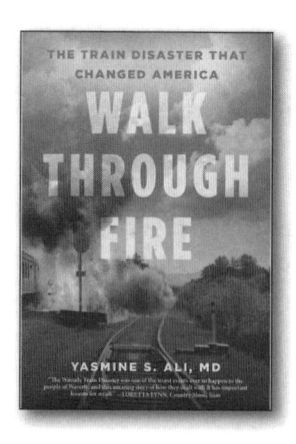

WALK THROUGH FIRE: THE TRAIN DISASTER THAT CHANGED AMERICA

Yasmine S. Ali, MD

The first book to examine the rarely-acknowledged Waverly Train Disaster of 1978—the catastrophic accident that changed America forever and led to the formation of FEMA. Coinciding with the 45th anniversary of the event, *Walk Through Fire* is a tribute to the first responders, as well as an examination of the strengths and vulnerabilities in rural America.

On the night of February 22, 1978, a devastating train explosion in the small town of Waverly, Tennessee could have been dismissed as a single community's terrible misfortune. Instead it became the catalyst for radical change, including the formation of FEMA, much-needed reforms in emergency response training, and the creation and enforcement of national and state safety regulations. Response to the disaster reshaped American infrastructure and laid the groundwork for the future of emergency management and disaster relief . . . and yet most Americans have never heard of Waverly.

Waverly native and award-winning medical writer Dr. Yasmine S. Ali draws from over a decade of meticulous research and interviews with survivors, first responders, and other firsthand accounts, including those of her own parents, first-generation Americans who were on call at the local hospital that treated the victims. Ali weaves a compelling narrative of small-town tragedy set against the broader backdrop of U.S. railroad history, rural healthcare, and other elements of American infrastructure that played a part in the creation—and the aftermath—of the Disaster.

"The Waverly Train Disaster was one of the worst events ever to happen to the people of Waverly and this amazing story of how they dealt with it has important lessons for all of us." —**Country music legend Loretta Lynn**

ABOUT THE AUTHOR: **Yasmine Ali, MD** is an award-winning medical writer, researcher, professor, and Waverly native. She can be found online at YasmineAliMD.com.

February 2023 | Hardcover | $28.00 | 9780806542188 | Citadel Press
July 2024 | Paperback | 16.95 | 9780806542195 | Citadel Press

CONVERSATION STARTERS

1. Yasmine Ali's descriptions of the Waverly train disaster are deeply descriptive, incorporating first-hand observations, emotions, and details that are often uncomfortable and shocking. Did reading this account make you think of any other contemporary or historical disasters?

2. FEMA, The Federal Emergency Management Agency, is one of many federal agencies that exist to provide regulatory oversight on behalf of the government. Did reading about how the Waverly Train Disaster became a catalyst for the formation of FEMA make you think about how those other agencies came into being? What are some examples of how other regulatory agencies play a role in improving society and individual health?

3. In a chapter devoted to her father – a surgeon on staff at the local hospital on the day of the train disaster – and other hospital staff, Ali illustrates their resilience, professionalism, and deep medical knowledge, attributes that were crucial in the hours after the fire. Does her depiction impact your impression of emergency workers, EMS, ER doctors and nurses?

4. Dr. Ali illustrates the US railway system's importance to the development and functioning of this country, as well as its many past and current problems. What did you learn about America's railway infrastructure, its history and its complexities?

5. Police Sergeant Elton "Toad" Smith, who was badly burned during the train explosion, endures and emerges from trauma. How does his long process of recovery – and his commitment to Waverly – make you feel about your own capacity to get through hard times?

6. *Walk Through Fire* addresses numerous disasters involving hazardous materials, from Chernobyl to Fukushima to an ammonium nitrate explosion in Beirut that devastated the entire country's economy. How do those accounts make you think about the people who handle hazardous materials every day?

7. Inspiring examples of leadership and heroism appear throughout the pages of *Walk Through Fire* as ordinary people facing chaotic, dire circumstances step up to help. What do these instances teach us about the nature of crisis and of human behavior?

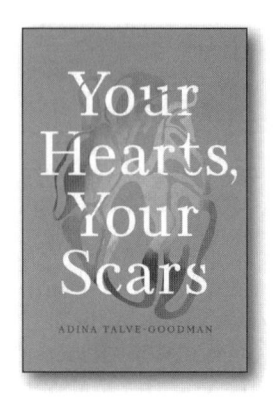

YOUR HEARTS, YOUR SCARS

Adina Talve-Goodman (Author), Sarika Talve-Goodman and Hannah Tinti (Editors), Jo Firestone (Foreword)

Engaging, funny, and unflinching essays about coming of age as a transplant patient and living each day as a gift.

Adina Talve-Goodman was born with a congenital heart condition and survived multiple operations over the course of her childhood, including a heart transplant at age nineteen. In these seven essays, she tells the story of her chronic illness and her youthful search for love and meaning, never forgetting that her adult life is tied to the loss of another person—the donor of her transplanted heart. Published posthumously, *Your Hearts, Your Scars* is the work of a writer wise beyond her years, a moving reflection on chance and gratitude, and a testament to hope and kindness.

"Adina Talve-Goodman walked a tightrope, for much of her thirty-one years, between life and death. Perhaps for this reason, Adina embodied life more than any person I've ever met. . . . [She] was a brilliant writer, and these pages are imbued with her exuberance, her sharp humor, and both versions of her spectacular heart." —**Ann Napolitano**, author of author of *Dear Edward*

"This book is so full of life that it's hard to believe the amazing young woman who wrote it is no longer walking among us. Adina has left an indelible mark on this world. Her extraordinary gifts, her irrepressible spirit, live on." —**Dani Shapiro**, author of *Inheritance* and *Signal Fires*

ABOUT THE AUTHOR: **Adina Talve-Goodman (1986-2018)** was born in St. Louis, graduated from Washington University, and performed internationally as an actress. She later became a mentor for Girls Write Now and the managing editor of the literary magazine *One Story*. She was diagnosed with a rare form of lymphoma, caused by post-transplant immunosuppressants, as she was attending the University of Iowa Nonfiction Writing Program and working on what would become her debut collection of essays *Your Hearts, Your Scars*.

January 2023 | Paperback | $17.99 | 9781954276055 | Bellevue Literary Press

CONVERSATION STARTERS

1. In the opening pages, Adina's friend, comedian Jo Firestone, writes, "Around her I laughed the hardest and cried the hardest. She fiercely reminded us how much we were loved." Were you able to get a sense of Adina as a person in these essays, beyond what her loved ones shared?

2. Adina describes being on the transplant list as "an exercise in how close you can get to death—close enough to earn a heart, not so close that the heart can't bring you back." How much did you know about how the transplant list works before reading this book? Do the factors considered seem just to you? What did Adina think about the justice of the process?

3. Adina explores what it means for her to live with illness, and also the ways others react to her body and her story. How do Adina's friends, lovers, strangers, and family see her body before and after her transplant? How do their reactions shape her understanding of herself?

4. At one point, Adina tells her father, a rabbi, about the man she met who had survived fourteen years with his transplant. She explains, "Sometimes the universe just shouts *I Got You*, y'know?" He responds, "That's like God." What does he mean? How does Adina's Jewish background and spirituality guide her through both illness and health?

5. Adina details several encounters with strangers in need: the man beside his toppled wheelchair, the man outside the café asking for money, the man who loved a dying woman. What does anyone owe to strangers? What does Adina choose to give them? Does empathy cost too much, or is it ultimately worth it?

6. When Adina finally receives her transplant, she worries about the responsibility and whether she deserves the heart. "What will I do with all that time?" she asks herself. "How will I ever be worthy of it?" Most of us have more time but rarely ask the same questions. What choices can we make to live up to our own hearts?

YOUNG ADULT

AN ARROW TO THE MOON

Emily X.R. Pan

Romeo and Juliet meets Chinese mythology in this magical novel by the *New York Times* bestselling author of *The Astonishing Color of After*.

Hunter Yee has perfect aim with a bow and arrow, but all else in his life veers wrong. He's sick of being haunted by his family's past mistakes. The only things keeping him from running away are his little brother, a supernatural wind, and the bewitching girl at his new high school.

Luna Chang dreads the future. Graduation looms ahead, and her parents' expectations are stifling. When she begins to break the rules, she finds her life upended by the strange new boy in her class, the arrival of unearthly fireflies, and an ominous crack spreading across the town of Fairbridge.

As Hunter and Luna navigate their families' enmity and secrets, everything around them begins to fall apart. All they can depend on is their love...but time is running out, and fate will have its way.

An Arrow to the Moon, Emily X.R. Pan's brilliant and ethereal follow-up to *The Astonishing Color of After*, is a story about family, love, and the magic and mystery of the moon that connects us all.

ABOUT THE AUTHOR: **Emily X.R. Pan** lives on Lenape land in Brooklyn, New York, but was originally born in the Midwestern United States to immigrant parents from Taiwan. Her debut novel, *The Astonishing Color of After*, was a *New York Times* bestseller, winner of the APALA Honor and Walter Honor awards, a finalist for the *L.A. Times Book* Prize, longlisted for the Carnegie Medal, and featured on over a dozen best-of-the-year lists. She received her MFA in fiction from the NYU Creative Writing Program, where she was a Goldwater Fellow and editor-in-chief of *Washington Square*. She was the founding editor-in-chief of *Bodega Magazine*, and went on to co-create the FORESHADOW platform and anthology.

April 2022 | Hardcover | $18.99 | 9780316464024 | Little, Brown Books for Young Readers
October 2023 | Paperback | $11.99 | 9780316464024 | Little, Brown Books for Young Readers

CONVERSATION STARTERS

1. *An Arrow to the Moon* is written from multiple perspectives. What did you learn from different characters' chapters? Was there a character that you responded to most strongly?

2. College represents different things for Hunter and Luna. What factors play into their opposing views of higher education? Do you relate to either of their sentiments? Think about your own views on college and try to identify what aspects of your life have shaped it.

3. While discussing college, Hunter tells Luna that she is practically an "Asian sheep" and following the herd mentality (170). What do you think he means by these words?

4. How do the relationships between parent and child vary between Luna's family and Hunter's family? What similarities and differences do you see?

5. Why do both families care so much about how the small Asian-identifying community of Fairbridge views them? How does their emphasis on 'saving face' impact family dynamics and their own evaluation of themselves?

6. How does the Yee family's fear of Rodney Wong manifest in their treatment of Hunter?

7. What is the significance of Hunter and Luna creating stories based on the lives of those around them? Why are they so opposed to fairytales?

8. Why does Luna become so upset when Hunter claims that Taiwanese and Chinese are virtually the same identity? How do their parents' thoughts and ideas inform their own beliefs? What does this argument make them realize, and how could they have discussed it differently?

9. What do different characters sacrifice? How do those sacrifices help others? How do they hurt?

10. The appearance of the crack in Fairbridge may have been literal, but can you ascribe any figurative meaning to its appearance in Luna and Hunter's lives? How does it tie to the beginning of the story?

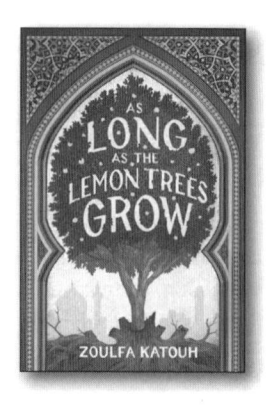

AS LONG AS THE LEMON TREES GROW

Zoulfa Katouh

A love letter to Syria and its people, *As Long as the Lemon Trees Grow* is a speculative novel set amid the Syrian Revolution, burning with the fires of hope, love, and possibility. Perfect for fans of *The Book Thief* and *Salt to the Sea*.

Salama Kassab was a pharmacy student when the cries for freedom broke out in Syria. She still had her parents and her big brother; she still had her home. She had a normal teenager's life.

Now Salama volunteers at a hospital in Homs, helping the wounded who flood through the doors daily. Secretly, though, she is desperate to find a way out of her beloved country before her sister-in-law, Layla, gives birth. So desperate, that she has manifested a physical embodiment of her fear in the form of her imagined companion, Khawf, who haunts her every move in an effort to keep her safe.

But even with Khawf pressing her to leave, Salama is torn between her loyalty to her country and her conviction to survive. Salama must contend with bullets and bombs, military assaults, and her shifting sense of morality before she might finally breathe free. And when she crosses paths with the boy she was supposed to meet one fateful day, she starts to doubt her resolve in leaving home at all.

Soon, Salama must learn to see the events around her for what they truly are—not a war, but a revolution—and decide how she, too, will cry for Syria's freedom.

ABOUT THE AUTHOR: **Zoulfa Katouh** is a Canadian with Syrian roots based in Switzerland. She is currently pursuing her master's in Drug Sciences and finds Studio Ghibli inspiration in the mountains, lakes, and stars surrounding her. When she's not talking to herself in the woodland forest, she's drinking iced coffee, baking aesthetic cookies and cakes, and telling everyone who would listen about how BTS paved the way. A dream of hers is to get Kim Nam-joon to read one of her books. *As Long as the Lemon Trees Grow* is her debut novel.

September 2022 | Hardcover | $18.99 | 9780316351379 | Little, Brown Books for Young Readers

CONVERSATION STARTERS

1. Layla says to Salama, "This revolution is about us getting our lives back. It's not about survival" (11). Do you agree? Why do you think revolutions happen?

2. Layla remarks, "This is not a war, Salama. It's a revolution" (12). What do you think the difference between the two is?

3. Khawf appeared to Salama after her mother was killed, and he only shows her the horrible things that have happened or that could happen. Why do you think he does that? What does he represent to Salama?

4. Salama is worried that every day could be her last, yet she is reluctant to leave Syria, even knowing it would be better for herself and Layla to leave. What do you believe is keeping her there?

5. How do you feel about Am charging thousands of dollars to desperate people wanting a better life?

6. Salama uses Am's wounded daughter against him to get passages for herself and Layla on a boat leaving Syria. Do you think that was the right thing for her to do?

7. Hamza makes Salama promise to take care of Layla, even though she is the younger sister. Do you think that was fair to Salama? Do you think it played a part in the break of Salama's mental health?

8. Kenan was ready to send his siblings out of Syria while he stayed behind. Discuss why you think he would have made that decision.

9. How do you think flowers help Salama find a moment of peace?

10. Kenan takes Salama to see the sunset and says they deserve to see the colors (199). Do you agree that it is important to see beauty even in the pain? Why or why not?

11. Kenan says to Salama, "There are enough people hurting you. Don't be one of them" (209). What do you think he means? How was Salama hurting herself?

12. What do you think lemons and lemon trees represent in the story?

13. *As Long as the Lemon Trees Grow* is a love story at its core. Who do you think it's a love story to?

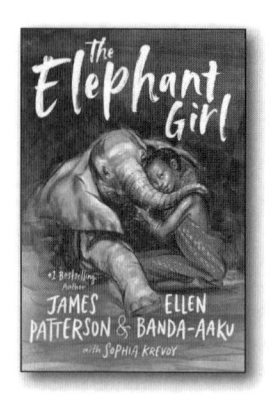

THE ELEPHANT GIRL

James Patterson & Ellen Banda-Aaku

#1 bestselling author James Patterson and award-winning author Ellen Banda-Aaku deliver an unforgettable story of a girl, an elephant, and their life-changing friendship—perfect for fans of *The One and Only Ivan*, *Pax*, and *Because of Winn-Dixie*.

Clever, sensitive Jama likes elephants better than people. While her classmates gossip—especially about the new boy, Leku—twelve-year-old Jama takes refuge at the watering hole outside her village. There she befriends a baby elephant she names Mbegu, Swahili for seed.

When Mbegu's mother, frightened by poachers, stampedes, Jama and Mbegu are blamed for two deaths—one elephant and one human. Now Leku, whose mysterious and imposing father is head ranger at the conservancy, may be their only lifeline.

Inspired by true events, *The Elephant Girl* is a moving exploration of the bonds between creatures and the power of belonging.

ABOUT THE AUTHORS: **James Patterson** is the world's bestselling author. The creator of *Max Einstein* and *Middle School*, he founded JIMMY Patterson to publish books that young readers will love. He lives in Florida with his family.

Ellen Banda-Aaku is an award-winning author and producer. She has lived, studied, and worked in Ghana, South Africa, and Zambia, and currently lives in the UK with her two children.

July 2022 | Hardcover | $16.99 | 9780316316927 | Little, Brown Books for Young Readers

CONVERSATION STARTERS

1. What is the most surprising fact you learned about elephants? Did the story inspire you to research more about endangered species? What other facts can you discover?

2. When describing the Eunoto ceremony, Jama explains how Maasai traditions have had to change over the years (8). Why might this cause tension in the community? Do you think it's important for traditions to evolve if necessary?

3. In chapter one, Jama speaks about conflicting emotions and her mother looking as though "two feelings were fighting within her" (4). How does this idea remain a consistent theme throughout the novel? In what other instances do characters face contrasting feelings?

4. The authors often describe the humans using animal comparisons such as, "delicate as a hummingbird", "just like a lion", "aggressive as a hippo", and "look like a spider" (13, 19, 24-25). Does this highlight the similarities between species? As much as it gives humans animalistic qualities, does it also help humanize the animals?

5. What does Mzee Naserian's proverb, "coal laughs at ashes not knowing the same fate will befall it" mean? (72-73) What do the proverbs symbolize, especially coming from an elder like Mzee Naserian? Why are they important?

6. Describe Jama's connection with Mbegu. How does it grow when they both experience loss? How do their journeys continue to mirror each other, all the way to the end of the novel?

7. Why is Jama so insistent that her mother's death is, "not the elephants' fault" (117)? How does this moment illustrate Jama's strength, and her compassion for all creatures?

8. In the airplane, Matthew's doubt in Jama's skills jeopardizes Mbegu's health. Why? How does Jama's confidence grow throughout the story? What has the biggest impact on her self-esteem?

9. How does Jama and Leku's relationship change over the course of the novel? Did you predict where they would end up? Why or why not?

10. The author's note speaks to the real-life threats to elephants that inspired the novel. What real-life lessons or messages did you take away from this fictional story?

FIGHT BACK

A. M. Dassu

Smash the patriarchy. Eat all the pastries.

Thirteen-year-old Aaliyah can't wait for a concert by her favorite K-pop boy band, 3W. She isn't too concerned with stories on the news about the rise of the far right—after all, it doesn't affect her—until a terrorist attack at the concert changes everything.

Local racists are emboldened and anti-Muslim rhetoric starts cropping up at school and on the street. When Aaliyah starts getting bullied, she knows she has to do something to stand up to the hate. She decides that, instead of hiding who she is, she will begin wearing a hijab for the first time, to challenge how people in her community see Muslims.

But when her school bans the hijab and she is attacked and intimidated for making her choice, Aaliyah feels alone. Can she find allies—friends to stand beside her and help her find ways to fight back?

Acclaimed author A. M. Dassu's follow-up to *Boy, Everywhere* is an essential read to encourage empathy, challenge stereotypes, and foster positive action.

"A powerful novel [that] will show readers they are not alone when facing racism and hate and that standing together in support of one another provides hope for the future." —*Booklist*

"This group of committed friends will win readers' hearts." —*Kirkus Reviews*

ABOUT THE AUTHOR: **A. M. Dassu** is the internationally acclaimed author of *Boy, Everywhere*, an ALA Notable Book which was also nominated for the Carnegie Medal and shortlisted for the Waterstone's Children's Book Prize. She won the We Need Diverse Books mentorship award in 2017 and serves on the Advisory Board of *SCBWI-British Isles' Words Pictures* magazine. She is a director at Inclusive Minds, an organization for people who are passionate about inclusion, diversity, equality, and accessibility in children's literature.

October 2022 | Hardcover | $21.95 | 9781643795881 | Lee & Low Books

CONVERSATION STARTERS

1. What does the title *Fight Back* mean to you after reading? Why do you think the author chose this particular title?

2. How does Aaliyah's find her identity throughout the story?

3. How does Aaliyah's character change and evolve from the beginning of the book versus the end of the book?

4. What do Aaliyah's friends throughout the book teach her?

5. Why does Mum not want Aaliyah to wear her hijab to school?

6. What lessons does Aaliyah learn about honesty and responsibility? What mistakes help her learn about what is important in life?

7. How does Aaliyah use her passion for freedom of expression and identity to fight for what she believes in? Who helps her in the fight against the religious symbols ban at school? What does this show you about the true meaning of friendship?

8. How does Aaliyah change her thinking on confronting those individuals who have caused her harm (Darren, Jayden, Sasha)?

9. What lesson(s) does Aaliyah realize at the end of the story?

10. What does family mean to you after reading this story? Have any of your perceptions or feelings toward family members changed after reading this book? How do Aaliyah's relationships with her family members inspire you to act toward your own family and friends?

11. Explore the structure of this text. Does the story describe events chronologically, as comparison, cause and effect, or problems and solutions? Why do you think the author structured the text the way she did?

12. How did you feel throughout the book? What thoughts and emotions did you experience as you read *Fight Back*? What did you learn about what is means to be an ally? How did this story connect to your life? What moments did you identify with? Why?

13. Read about author is A. M. Dassu's life (amdassu.com). What inspired her to write this story? How can our own lives and experiences be mined for inspiration? How can real life be used in fiction writing?

MERCI SUÁREZ PLAYS IT COOL

Meg Medina

Newbery Medalist Meg Medina follows Merci Suárez into a year full of changes—evolving friendships, new responsibilities, and heartbreaking loss.

For Merci Suárez, eighth grade means a new haircut, nighttime football games, and an out-of-town overnight field trip. At home, it means more chores and keeping an eye on Lolo as his health worsens. It's a year filled with more responsibility and independence, but also with opportunities to reinvent herself. Merci has always been fine with not being one of the popular kids like Avery Sanders, who is always traveling to fun places and buying new clothes. But then Avery starts talking to Merci more, and not just as a teammate. Does this mean they're friends? Merci wants to play it cool, but with Edna always in her business, it's only a matter of time before Merci has to decide where her loyalty stands. Whether Merci is facing school drama or changing family dynamics, readers will empathize as she discovers who she can count on—and what can change in an instant.

"Pitch-perfect dialogue capture[s] the angst of adolescence with honesty and respect." —*School Library Journal* (starred review)

"Well-crafted dialogue, humor, and cultural exploration [that] readers expect. A fabulous finale to a memorable trilogy." —*Kirkus Reviews* (starred review)

"This final entry in the Merci Suárez trilogy once again shows readers the strength and beauty of family." —*Booklist* (starred review)

"The strength of this story lies in the authenticity of Merci's character and her refreshingly sincere responses to the world around her." —*The Horn Book* (starred review)

ABOUT THE AUTHOR: **Meg Medina** is the author of the Newbery Medal winner and Kirkus Prize finalist *Merci Suárez Changes Gears* and its sequel, *Merci Suárez Can't Dance*, as well as several award-winning young adult novels and picture books.

September 2023 | Paperback | $8.99 | 9781536233001 | Candlewick Press

CONVERSATION STARTERS

1. Family is a huge part of Merci's life. How does the change in family dynamics throughout the book affect her? Consider the growth that different family members make and the forgiveness needed between the different relations and generations.

2. On page 54, Roli downloads the audiobooks of Merci's summer reading texts, and Merci asks, "Is this allowed?" Audiobooks have been found to have the same benefits as reading when it comes to comprehension and analysis. Do you believe that audiobooks count as reading? Why or why not?

3. When Mrs. Ransome is told Roli is going to school to be a doctor (60-61), her reaction is one of surprise. Why is Merci so offended by her reaction? What does the reaction tell us about preconceived notions and societal racism?

4. When Lolo runs away from the house, Papi's first reaction, after he is found, is to be angry (69). Why do you think Papi reacts this way? What is Roli's reaction? Compare the two responses and discuss whether one is the better choice for the situation.

5. How does Merci compare boa constrictors shedding to 8th graders (92)? Do you agree with the comparison?

6. Guidance and guidance groups play a large part in Merci's story. Why do you think it is hard for Merci to open up to the guidance counselor? Do you think the connection she makes is ultimately helpful?

7. Grief is an all-encompassing emotion. How does it affect Merci? Why is the idea of a way forward (307) so devastating for Merci?

THE SILENCE THAT BINDS US

Joanna Ho

Joanna Ho, *New York Times* bestselling author of *Eyes That Kiss in the Corners*, has written an exquisite, heart-rending debut young adult novel that will inspire all to speak truth to power.

Maybelline Chen isn't the Chinese Taiwanese American daughter her mother expects her to be. May prefers hoodies over dresses and wants to become a writer. When asked, her mom can't come up with one specific reason for why she's proud of her only daughter. May's beloved brother, Danny, on the other hand, has just been admitted to Princeton. But Danny secretly struggles with depression, and when he dies by suicide, May's world is shattered.

In the aftermath, racist accusations are hurled against May's parents for putting too much "pressure" on him. May's father tells her to keep her head down. Instead, May challenges these ugly stereotypes through her writing. Yet the consequences of speaking out run much deeper than anyone could foresee. Who gets to tell our stories, and who gets silenced? It's up to May to take back the narrative.

"An ornately carved window into the core of shared humanity. Read and re-read. Then read it again." —**Nic Stone**, *New York Times* **bestselling author of** *Dear Martin*

"A held-breath of a novel that finds courage amidst brokeness, and holds a candle to the dark." —**Stacey Lee**, *New York Times* **bestselling author of** *The Downstairs Girl*

ABOUT THE AUTHOR: **Joanna Ho** is the *New York Times* bestselling author of *Eyes that Kiss in the Corners*, *Eyes that Speak to the Stars*, *Playing at the Border: A Story of Yo-Yo Ma*, and *The Silence that Binds Us*. She has been an English teacher, a dean, a professional development mastermind, and a high school vice principal. Her passion for equity in books and education is matched only by her love of homemade chocolate chip cookies, outdoor adventures, and dance parties with her kids.

June 2022 | Hardcover | $17.99 | 9780063059344 | HarperTeen

CONVERSATION STARTERS

1. Maybelline Chen isn't the Chinese Taiwanese American daughter her mother expects her to be. What are the rules, implicit and explicit, that May identifies her mother having for her?

2. May's beloved brother Danny secretly struggles with depression. What are some ways we as a community might address mental health in an honest and supportive way?

3. May's story is ultimately one of healing, after the tragedy of her brother Danny's death. Is there a time in your life when friends and family have helped you heal?

4. May's friendship with Tiya and Marc is essential to May's journey toward self-awareness and discovery, and explores Black and Asian solidarity—what does this mean to you?

5. "We will never have a better world until all our stories are told. We will never have a better world until all our histories are known. We will never have a better world until all our voices are heard." How are those themes explored in the novel?

6. May experiences anti-Asian racism and learns to use her voice to combat it. Have you ever experienced racism? How might you help to speak out against it?

7. Have you ever felt silenced or made to feel invisible? What do you think the title, "The Silence that Binds Us" means?

8. May's writing gives her the strength to be brave, to fight against injustice, and to take back the narrative. What is it about writing that makes May feel brave? How have you used your voice to help others?

9. Look at the cover. What symbolism do you see there?

10. May learns there is a cost that comes from speaking out. And there is a cost that comes from staying silent. How do we know the right path forward if every choice requires sacrifice?

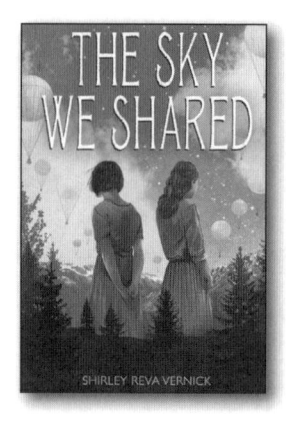

THE SKY WE SHARED

Shirley Reva Vernick

In southern Japan, Tamiko spends her time writing in her diary, dreaming of making theatrical costumes, and praying her brother Kyo makes it back from the war. She wishes she could be brave like him and help the war effort.

In rural Oregon, Nellie spends her time lying in the grass, studying the stars, and wishing for her pa to return from the war. She also wishes the boy next door, Joey, would talk to her again like he used to.

Soon the girls' lives become inextricably linked.

Tamiko and her classmates are brought to a damp, repurposed theater to make large paper balloons to help the military.

No one knows what they are for.

Nellie and her classmates ration food, work in salvage drives, and support their community.

No one knows what's coming.

"[An] engrossing novel." —*The Horn Book*, **starred review**

"Balanced narratives and steady pacing effectively highlight an often-overlooked period in both Japanese and American history." —***Publishers Weekly*, starred review**

ABOUT THE AUTHOR: **Shirley Reva Vernick** is an award winning author and journalist. Her previous works include *The Blood Lie*, *Remember Dippy*, and *The Black Butterfly*. Her interviews and feature articles have appeared in numerous magazines, national newspapers, and university publications. She also runs a popular storytelling website, storybee.org, which is used in schools, libraries, hospitals, and homes all over the world. Vernick graduated from Cornell University and is an alumna of the Radcliffe Writing Seminars. She lives in Amherst, Massachusetts.

June 2022 | Hardcover | $22.95 | 9781947627529 | Lee & Low Books

CONVERSATION STARTERS

1. Compare Tamiko and Nellie as characters. Why do you think the author chose to include the perspectives from both Nellie and Tamiko in *The Sky We Shared*?

2. Discuss the perceptions of Japanese and American people from both Tamiko and Nellie's perspectives. How do their thought processes change throughout the book?

3. Examine the relationships that Tamiko and Nellie have with their families in *The Sky We Shared*. How are their families impacted by the war?

4. How do Tamiko and Nellie support the war effort? What do they learn about the war when the begin to help with the war effort?

5. How are Tamiko and Nellie's friendships affected by the war? What are some of the ways that they must navigate relationships with their friends throughout the book?

6. What is the author's message about war's human cost? What do you think Shirley Reva Vernick wanted to impart on the reader about the impacts of World War II?

7. Joey Cooper is angry that his older brother died in battle. He directs this anger toward the returning Japanese Americans. Why do you think he does this?

8. What is the role of propaganda in the book? How are these themes relevant in our society today?

9. Compare and contrast each of their home environments and the effects on them mentally and physically.

10. What is the role of "enemy" in *The Sky We Shared*? What is an "enemy" to Tamiko? To Nellie? How does the concept of "enemy" evolve?

11. How does violence and death from the war impact both Tamiko and Nellie?

12. What do Tamiko and Nellie both come to understand at the conclusion of the book?

13. Why do you think Shirley Reva Vernick wanted to write about civilians experiencing the devastation of enemy weapons? How does it make you think about historical events that are traditionally taught and the facts that are often omitted?

SNITCHERS

Stephane Dunn

Nia Barnes is preparing to enter high school and trying to stay on her mama's good side. Life in her small Midwestern city hasn't been the same since her father's unsolved murder, driving Nia's love of detective novels and true crime stories.

When the little boy she babysits is caught in the crossfire of a drive-by shooting, Nia and her best friends Dontay and Miracle Ruth secretly set out to get him justice. They look up police reports and listen to the conversations of their elders; they try to follow suspects the way Nia's favorite teen detectives might.

But the search for truth isn't straightforward, especially when you're somewhere between being kids and adults, and people want peace but are afraid to talk.

Writer and filmmaker Stephane Dunn makes her YA debut with this endearing, heart-wrenching novel about loss, truth, and the reality of violence in communities everywhere.

"Authentic, complex, and compelling friendships lie at the heart of this timely novel. A thrilling story grounded in a thoughtful exploration of social themes."
—*Kirkus Reviews*

ABOUT THE AUTHOR: **Stephanie Dunn** is a writer, filmmaker and professor. Her work has appeared in *The Atlantic*, *Vogue*, *Ms.* magazine, *Chronicle of Higher Education*, CNN.com, *The Root*, and *Best African American Essays 2009*, among others. She is the author of *Baad Bitches & Sassy Supermamas: Black Power Action Films*, and the Tirota/Finish Line Social Impact Script Competition award-winning screenplay, *Chicago '66*. She lives in Atlanta, Georgia, with her family.

September 2022 | Hardcover | $20.95 | 9781947627635 | Lee & Low Books

CONVERSATION STARTERS

1. How does Nia's father's death change the way she looks at life?

2. How does Nia process Little Petey's death? How does Nia describe her pain when she thinks about Little Petey?

3. What is Nia's relationship with her mother like? How do we see the relationship with her mother change over time?

4. How do the Nancy Drew novels inspire Nia?

5. Why do you think Dontay is so worried about being labeled as a "snitch"? Why is it important for Nia to breakdown what it means to be a snitch?

6. What role does religion play in Nia's life?

7. How does Nia use her pen pal relationship with Alima to help deal with the trauma of losing Little Petey? What connection(s) does she share with her pen pal?

8. How has violence and gun violence affected Nia's family and community? What does gun violence look like across the United States? What does violence look like across the world?

9. What do you notice about how Nia describes the death of her grandfather, her dad and Little Petey?

10. What message does Reverend Don King deliver at Little Petey's funeral? Why is this message so powerful?

11. What is special about the relationship between Nia and Nana Mae?

12. Why do you think it was important for Nia, her mother and Nana Mae to seek counseling? What is powerful about the author talking about going to therapy?

13. Why do Nia and her friends decide to do a film on "Stop the violence"?

14. What role does the community play in *Snitchers*? How does Little Petey's death bring together the community?

15. What relationship does the police have with the community?

16. What does the title *Snitchers* mean to you after reading? Why do you think the author chose this particular title?

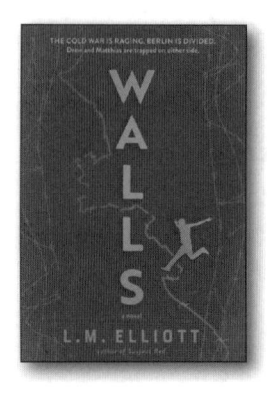

WALLS

L.M. Elliott

Drew is an army brat in West Berlin, where soldiers like his dad hold an outpost of democracy against communist Russia. Drew's cousin Matthias, an East Berliner, has grown up in the wreckage of Allied war bombing, on streets ruled by the secret police.

From enemy sides of this Cold War standoff, the boys become wary friends, arguing over the space race, politics, even civil rights, but bonding over music. If informants catch Matthias with rock 'n' roll records or books Drew has given him, he could be sent to a work camp. If Drew gets too close to an East Berliner, others on the army post may question his family's loyalty. As the political conflict around them grows dire, Drew and Matthias are tested in ways that will change their lives forever.

Set in the tumultuous year leading up to the surprise overnight raising of the Berlin Wall in August 1961, and illustrated with dozens of real-life photographs of the time, *Walls* brings to vivid life a heroic and tragic episode of the Cold War.

"Immersive . . . An expertly crafted, evocative time capsule." —**Publishers Weekly, starred review**

"Elliott both fills in the historical background—aided by Behm's mixing of period photos, contemporary news, and pop-culture notes—and crafts a tale of rising tensions that culminates in a suspenseful climax . . . A sensitive exploration of cogent themes in a richly detailed historical setting." —**Kirkus Reviews, starred review**

"The portrayal of events is first-rate, creating a poignant yet lighthearted read." —**Booklist**

ABOUT THE AUTHOR: **L.M. Elliott** was an award-winning magazine journalist in Washington, D.C., before becoming a *New York Times* bestselling author of historical and biographical young adult novels. Her other works include *Under a War-Torn Sky*, *Suspect Red*, and *Hamilton and Peggy*.

February 2023 | Paperback | $10.99 | 9781643753515 | Algonquin Young Readers

CONVERSATION STARTERS

1. Both the Soviet and U.S. governments made use of propaganda during the Cold War. How does the era's political climate affect Drew's daily life? Where does he get information that shapes his ideas and opinions? How does he evaluate the information he gets? How is that similar to or different from the ways Matthias gets information?

2. The First Amendment to the U.S. Constitution protects the freedom of speech and expression against all levels of government censorship, allowing individuals in the United States to speak, publish, read, and view whatever they wish. But some institutions may remove or restrict access to certain works. What are some books or music that have been removed or restricted in U.S. locations? What else do you see being censored in *Walls* and in your own community? What is censorship really about?

3. Use Drew and Matthias to reflect on the relationship between the individual and society, and how that relationship is both influenced by and influences personal identity. Then consider and discuss how societal institutions—such as schools, governments, religions, or clubs, for example—your experiences within them, and other people's perceptions of who you are directly impact your identity. How do your experiences and identity affect your behavior and how you relate to those around you?

4. Drew's mom tells him she thinks that Shirley "even changed you a little for the better." What perspectives did Shirley bring to Drew? Who are the people in your life that get you to look closely at the world and think about what's happening around you?

5. L. M. Elliott tells a heroic and tragic story against a vivid historical backdrop. How did you decide what is historically true and what is fiction—the author's interpretation of historical events and facts and how those events would affect and influence her characters? In what ways are the issues of the era, such as prejudice, racism, and disinformation campaigns, relevant to us today? How has this novel affected the way you think about freedom and human rights?

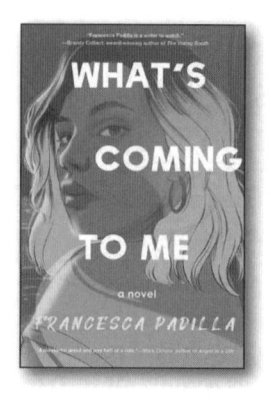

WHAT'S COMING TO ME
Francesca Padilla

In the seaside town of Nautilus, Minerva Gutiérrez absolutely hates her job at the local ice cream stand, where her sexist boss makes each day worse than the last. But she needs the money: kicked out of school and stranded by her mom's most recent hospitalization, she dreams of escaping her dead-end hometown. When an armed robbery at the ice cream stand stirs up rumors about money hidden on the property, Min teams up with her neighbor CeCe, also desperate for cash, to find it. The bonus? Getting revenge on her boss in the process.

If Minerva can do things right for once—without dirty cops, suspicious co-workers, and an ill-timed work crush getting in her way—she might have a way out . . . as long as the painful truths she's been running from don't catch up to her first.

"Padilla adroitly navigates issues of uncertainty, revenge, and sorrow in the straits of late adolescence with her Minerva's rebellion against a sexist and abusive boss and her search for some beauty and meaning in a life that seems to be coming apart at the seams." —*Oprah Daily*

"Raw and unflinching . . . A beautiful story about the uncertainty of adolescence, the burden of grief, and all the ways love can surprise you." —**Brandy Colbert**, award-winning author of *The Voting Booth*

"A masterful debut and one hell of a ride." —**Mark Oshiro**, author of *Anger is a Gift*

"Unexpected and suspenseful" —**Isabel Quintero**, author of *Gabi, Girl in Pieces*

ABOUT THE AUTHOR: **Francesca Padilla** is a Dominican-American fiction writer born and raised in New York City. She is the recipient of a Walter Dean Myers Grant from We Need Diverse Books and holds a BA in Creative Writing from the State University of New York at Purchase College. She lives with her family in Rochester, New York.

July 2023 | Paperback | $10.99 | 9781641294867 | Soho Teen

CONVERSATION STARTERS

1. How does Minerva process grief throughout the novel? How do strong emotions express themselves in surprising ways and actions for Minerva as well as secondary characters?

2. In what ways is Minerva a reliable narrator? In what ways is she not a reliable narrator?

3. What effect does the robbery have on Minerva?

4. Both Minerva and CeCe bring up the film *Scarface*. Compare Minerva's journey in *What's Coming to Me* to another character from a book, movie, or TV show.

5. Friendship is an important theme in *What's Coming to Me*. At the beginning of the novel, Minerva is estranged from her best friend, Mary. Why do you think this is the case? How does their friendship change over the course of the book? How would you describe Minerva's friendship with CeCe?

6. Anger is another important theme. What role does anger play in Minerva's character?

7. Describe Minerva's emotional journey. What feelings did you experience while reading the novel?

8. What do you think of the title of the book? How does that relate to the book itself, and what deeper meanings does it carry?

9. Share a favorite quote. Why did this resonate with you? How does it resonate with the character(s)?

BOOK GROUP FAVORITES FROM 2021

We asked thousands of book groups to tell us what books they read and discussed during 2020 that they enjoyed most. The top titles were:

FICTION

Nothing to See Here
Kevin Wilson | Ecco

The Last Flight
Julie Clark | Sourcebooks

Lady Clementine
Marie Benedict | Sourcebooks

The Four Winds
Kristin Hannah | St. Martin's Press

My Dark Vanessa
Kate Russell | William Morrow

Cilka's Journey
Heather Morris | St. Martin's Griffin

When the Apricots Bloom
Gina Wilkinson | Kensington Books

The Book Woman of Troublesome Creek
Kim Richardson | Sourcebooks

Hamnet
Maggie O'Farrell | Vintage

The Southern Book Club's Guide to Slaying Vampires
Grady Hendrix | Quirk

The Midnight Library
Matt Haig | Viking

Afterlife
Julia Alvarez | Algonquin

NONFICTION

The Yellow House
Sarah M. Bloom | Grove Press

Women Rowing North
Mary Pipher | Bloomsbury

Caste
Isabel Wilkerson | Random House

Stamped
Jason Reynolds | LBYR

The Woman They Could Not Silence
Kate Moore | Sourcebooks

Hidden Valley Road
Robert Kolker | Anchor

Educated
Tara Westover | Random House

The Radium Girls
Kate Moore | Sourcebooks

Real Estate
Deborah Levy | Bloomsbury

Me and White Supremacy
Layla F. Saad | Sourcebooks

YOUNG ADULT

Firekeeper's Daughter
Angeline Boulley | Henry Holt (BYR)

The Watsons Go To Birmingham- 1963
Christopher Paul Curtis | Yearling

The Fountains of Silence
Ruta Sepetys | Philomel Books

The Hate U Give
Angie Thomas | Balzer + Bray

All Thirteen
Christina Soontornvat | Candlewick

They Went Left
Monica Hesse | LBYR

Mad, Bad & Dangerous to Know
Samira Ahmed | Soho Teen

Black Brother, Black Brother
Jewell Parker Rhodes | LBYR

Please visit ReadingGroupChoices.com between January 1 and April 1, 2023 to enter our 2022 Favorite Books Contest by telling us about your favorite books of 2022. You will be entered for a chance to win bookstore gift certificates to use toward your meetings plus books for each person in your group, compliments of our publishing partners.

READING GROUP CHOICES

Selections for Lively Discussions

GUIDELINES FOR LIVELY BOOK DISCUSSIONS

1. RESPECT SPACE - Avoid "crosstalk" or talking over others.
2. ALLOW SPACE - Some of us are more outgoing and others more reserved. If you've had a chance to talk, allow others time to offer their thoughts as well.
3. BE OPEN - Keep an open mind, learn from others, and acknowlege there are differences in opinon. That's what makes it interesting!
4. OFFER NEW THOUGHTS - Try not to repeat what others have said, but offer a new perspective.
5. STAY ON THE TOPIC - Contribute to the flow of conversation by holding your comments to the topic of the book, keeping personal references to an appropriate medium.

Great Books ⁓ Great People ⁓ Great Conversation

DO YOU LOVE TO READ?

Spread the joy of reading and build a sense of community by starting a Little Free Library book exchange!

Hailed by the *New York Times* as "a global sensation", Little Free Library book exchanges are "take a book, return a book" gathering places where neighbors share their favorite literature and stories.

LITTLE FREE LIBRARY.ORG
TAKE A BOOK • RETURN A BOOK

Find locations near you and learn how to start your own at *www.littlefreelibrary.org*

INTRODUCING THE NEXT GREAT AUTHOR

Indies Introduce.
It's what independent booksellers have been doing forever – discovering and championing new authors.

INDIES Introduce

See titles at
BookWeb.org/indiesintroduce

READING GROUP CHOICES

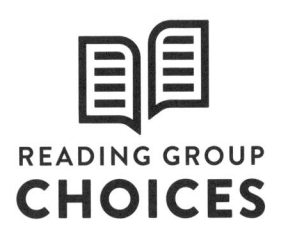

READING GROUP CHOICES' ADVISORY BOARD

Donna Paz Kaufman founded Reading Group Choices in 1994 to connect publishers, booksellers, libraries, and readers with great books for group discussion. Today, Paz & Associates owns Story & Song Bookstore Bistro and continues to assist people around the globe open, manage, and sell their independent bookstores in The Bookstore Training Group. To learn more about Paz & Associates, visit PazBookBiz.com.

John Mutter is editor-in-chief of *Shelf Awareness*, the daily e-mail newsletter focusing on books, media about books, retailing and related issues to help booksellers, librarians and others do their jobs more effectively. Before he and his business partner, Jenn Risko, founded the company in May 2005, he was executive editor of bookselling at *Publishers Weekly*. He has covered book industry issues for 25 years and written for a variety of publications, including *The Bookseller* in the U.K.; *Australian Bookseller & Publisher*; *Boersenblatt*, the German book trade magazine; and *College Store Magazine* in the U.S. For more information about *Shelf Awareness*, go to its website, shelf-awareness.com.

Kathy Schultenover has been a bookseller for 30 years. She started the reading groups at Nashville's Davis Kidd Booksellers in 1993, and facilitated a Classics Club, a Woman's Book Club, and the DK Book Club for contemporary fiction and nonfiction. She also started a Book Club Registry for local clubs. Until the store closed in 2010, she produced annual Book Club Workshops on a variety of topics of interest to community reading groups. In 2011 she joined the new Parnassus Books and has continued her role as Book Clubs Manager, leading in-store groups, holding workshops and speaking to groups throughout Nashville.

Charlie Mead owned and managed Reading Group Choices from 2005 until 2014. He sold the business to Mary Morgan in April 2014. Charlie's business partner and wife, Barbara Drummond Mead, co-owned and managed the business until her passing in 2011. From 1972 to 1999, Charlie served at Digital Equipment Corporation (DEC) and Compaq Computer Corporation, both now part of Hewlett Packard, most recently as vice president of communication accounts worldwide. In 1999, Charlie became vice president of Sales of Interpath Communications Corporation, an Internet infrastructure company, until the company's sale in 2000. From 2000 to 2005, Charlie owned and managed Connxsys LLC, a communications consulting firm.

Scott Onak served as the Communications Coordinator for Reading Group Choices from 2017-2021. He is a writer and educator who has taught creative writing at the University of Idaho, University of Chicago, and Story Studio Chicago, among other schools. His fiction has been published in journals including *Ninth Letter, Mid-American Review, Necessary Fiction,* and *Midwest Gothic,* and he has received writing residencies from Vermont Studio Center and the Ragdale Foundation. He currently lives and teaches English in France.

READING GROUP CHOICES ANNUAL GUIDES

Fiction, nonfiction, and young adult book recommendations
are included in each annual edition.

Order online at www.ReadingGroupChoices.com

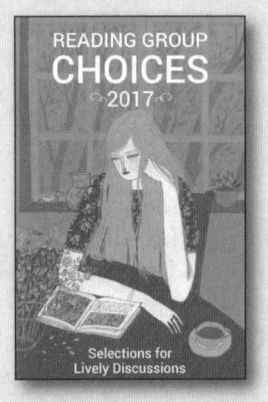

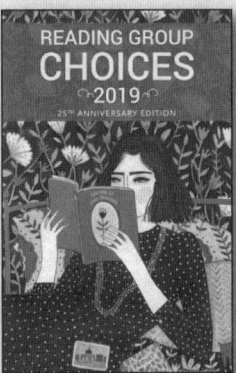

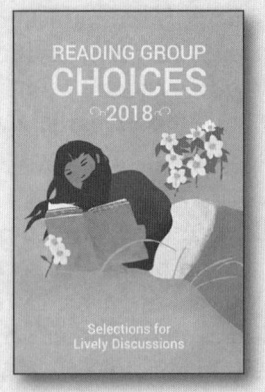

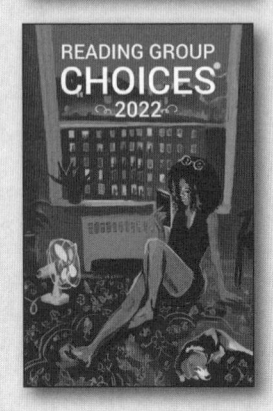